Dietrich
Bonhoeffer

WOMEN OF FAITH SERIES

Amy Carmichael   Harriet Tubman
Catherine Marshall   Isobel Kuhn
Corrie ten Boom   Joni Eareckson Tada
Fanny Crosby   Madame Guyon
Florence Nightingale   Mary Slessor
Gladys Aylward   Susanna Wesley

MEN OF FAITH SERIES

Andrew Murray   Jim Elliot
Billy Graham   John Calvin
Borden of Yale   John Hyde
Brother Andrew   John Newton
C. S. Lewis   John Paton
Charles Colson   John Wesley
Charles Finney   Jonathan Edwards
Charles Spurgeon   Jonathan Goforth
D. L. Moody   Luis Palau
David Brainerd   Martin Luther
Dietrich Bonhoeffer   Oswald Chambers
E. M. Bounds   Samuel Morris
Eric Liddell   William Booth
George Müller   William Carey
Hudson Taylor

WOMEN AND MEN OF FAITH

John and Betty Stam
Francis and Edith Schaeffer

OTHER BIOGRAPHIES FROM BETHANY HOUSE

Autobiography of Charles Finney (Wessel)
Behind the Stories (Eble)
Janette Oke: A Heart for the Prairie (Logan)
Jesus Freaks (dc Talk)
Jesus Freaks Vol. II (dc Talk)
Miracle in the Mirror (Buntain)
Of Whom the World Was Not Worthy (Chapian)
Out of Mormonism (Robertson)
Where Does a Mother Go to Resign? (Johnson)

Dietrich
Bonhoeffer

Susan Martins Miller

BETHANY HOUSE PUBLISHERS
MINNEAPOLIS, MINNESOTA 55438

Published by Bethany House Publishers
A Ministry of Bethany Fellowship International
11400 Hampshire Avenue South
Bloomington, Minnesota 55438
www.bethanyhouse.com

Printed in the United States of America by
Bethany Press International, Bloomington, Minnesota 55438

Library of Congress Cataloging-in-Publication Data

Miller, Susan Martins.
    Dietrich Bonhoeffer : the life and martyrdom of a great
man who counted the cost of discipleship / by Susan Martins
Miller.
        p.   cm. — (Men of faith)
Includes bibliographical references.
    ISBN 0-7642-2633-9 (pbk.)
1. Bonhoeffer, Dietrich, 1906-1945. I. Title. II. Series.
    BX4827.B57   M55   2002

                                        2002008647

Contents

1

Roots and Early Influences

In the early years of a new century, horses draped in black and drawing a hearse clip-clopped slowly down the road and turned into the graveyard. Mourners followed in black carriages or on foot. They had come to see a loved one laid to rest in the Catholic cemetery in Breslau, in eastern Germany.

From the house across the street, four young, curious eyes watched the procession. This was not the first time the two children had watched from the window, fascinated, as a funeral procession observed with traditional ceremony the passing of another citizen. Twins Dietrich and Sabine Bonhoeffer, still preschoolers, jumped at every chance to watch funeral processions along the river opposite their home. Later they would lie in the dark, squeeze their eyes shut, and concentrate on the word *eternity* as they imagined what death must be like.

For the first six years of Dietrich Bonhoeffer's life, he lived across the street from the Catholic cemetery in this house, where he had been born and where his older brothers and sisters also had entered the world. Although Breslau was not a large city and was a good distance away from political centers such as Berlin, the Bonhoeffer home was never a quiet place. Along with his twin sister, Dietrich had five older siblings and one younger sister. Eight Bonhoeffer children kept the household bustling. Karl-Friedrich, Walter, and Klaus were the "three big boys." Ursula and Christel were "the girls." From the time of their birth, Dietrich and Sabine were "the twins." Three years after them baby sister Susanne joined the family.

In the years before World War I, the Bonhoeffers were a well-to-do, patriotic, German Christian family. They maintained a winter home and a summer home. In addition to the large family, their household always included a governess for the older children and a nurse for the little ones. A housemaid, parlor maid, and cook looked after the housework. At times Dietrich's father also employed a receptionist and a chauffeur.

Paula Bonhoeffer, Dietrich's mother, was an independent spirit undaunted by challenges that made others shirk. She had learned by example. Her grandfather was a famous German church historian. Her own father had pursued wide-ranging interests in theology, history, and the visual arts. He served as a military chaplain and then as a professor of theology. Paula grew up participating freely in discussions with intellectual people who in turn sparked her intellectual development. She spoke her mind, and she did what she believed was right, even if others around her did not agree. At an age when girls usually were expected to stop their own schooling and concentrate on running a household, Paula took the qualifying examination for women teachers. She passed and became a certified teacher, putting this training to work as soon as she had children of her own. One large room in the Bonhoeffer home was furnished as a classroom, and here she gave most of her children their first lessons. Paula surrounded her offspring with an environment that stimulated their learning and curiosity about the world. Because of the excellent start that she gave them, several of the Bonhoeffer children were able to skip entire grades and take graduation examinations at remarkably young ages. Dietrich was one of these.

Paula Bonhoeffer was strict but full of imagination. The family home saw a steady stream of games, feasts, puppet shows, books, and parties. The Bonhoeffer parties became famous in the family's circle of friends because of Paula's spirited, creative themes. She always had a special game to play at a party, or a dance to teach, or amusing skits to present. As the children grew up and became accomplished musicians, they performed at their mother's gatherings.[1] Paula did not see herself as restricted to running a household for the sake of her husband's career. Her children did not grow up seeing her cooking or sewing but rather deeply involved in intense discussions about politics and church situations, holding forth her own opinions in the midst of changing political times.

Karl Bonhoeffer, Dietrich's father, came from a line of theologians, doctors, and lawyers. He was quieter than his wife, with a more reserved personality. He taught his children by example and manner rather than a gush of words. But his children knew and respected his authority. At the Bonhoeffer home, a mere raised eyebrow commanded a great deal. If Mama said, "Papa would not like that," behavior or ambitions changed accordingly. Karl's chosen profession was psychiatry, and he excelled at it. He was a premier German psychiatrist in the early decades of the twentieth century.

Dietrich and Sabine arrived at the family home in Breslau on February 4, 1906. Dietrich was ten minutes older than his sister, and he seldom missed an opportunity during their childhood to remind her of it. As twins often are, Dietrich and Sabine were very close, joyfully sharing every experience, until the custom of sending boys and girls to different schools took them down different paths. As Lutheran children curious about the Catholic cemetery across the street, they could not know the significance of the deep questions they explored together or the desperate decisions they would both face as adults.

When Dietrich and Sabine were six years old, their father was appointed to a professorship at the university in Berlin. They could not have understood the importance of this appointment for their father's career, but it changed their lives. Karl Bonhoeffer now held the most important university position in the field of psychiatry and neurology in all of Germany. Berlin was a long way from Breslau. At Eastertime 1912, the family moved from an outlying provincial town to the busy capital city of a changing Germany. They settled in an area of the city where many people had connections to the university. Now the children heard academic and political discussions even more often. The move tore up many early roots for Dietrich, but as the new family home became a meeting place for a wider circle of friends and acquaintances, all the Bonhoeffer children were exposed to intellectual and theological perspectives of a Germany that would soon change its face to the world.

2

Life-Changing Decisions

D ietrich's cry pierced the air. His siblings jumped up, alarmed. In seconds they saw what Dietrich saw and joined his cry. At the family summer home, Fraulein Lenchen, their teacher, flailed in the center of the lake, while the Bonhoeffer children looked on from shore, helpless to save her. They were under strict orders from the governess, Fraulein Horn, to wait until she gave permission to go swimming. They obeyed without question. But Fraulein Lenchen ran ahead. Enjoying the summer day, she headed straight into the water. She quickly reached the center of the lake—where she began to sink. Seven-year-old Dietrich was the first to notice and cry for help.

Fraulein Horn sprang into action. Though she was dressed in a woolen skirt that would soon be weighted by the water, she flung herself into the lake and swam to Fraulein Lenchen. The children watched anxiously from shore as their governess pulled their teacher back to dry ground. "Help me, dear God, help me!" Fraulein Horn cried. Fraulein Lenchen was unconscious. As Fraulein Horn put her fingers down her friend's throat to force out the water, Dietrich patted her back. At last Fraulein Lenchen coughed and revived, bringing a sigh of relief to everyone. Fraulein Horn said a long prayer of thanksgiving, and the day was etched into the memories of the Bonhoeffer children.[1]

Upon their move to Berlin, the Bonhoeffers settled into a pleasant house not far from Karl Bonhoeffer's work. He was the director of a mental hospital as well as professor of psychiatry and neurology at the university. The house was surrounded by large gardens, where the children endlessly played and dug caves. The family enjoyed a second home in Friedrichsbrunn in the eastern Harz Mountains. They could easily reach this seasonal place of rest and relief from Berlin and enjoyed long summer holidays there. It was at this home that Dietrich saw his governess save his teacher from drowning in the lake. The mountains and woods surrounding the house were an unending adventure for Dietrich and Sabine. As they explored, they could hunt for mushrooms or gather berries or imagine anything they wanted.

When Dietrich was eight, he discovered the joys of music. The entire family was musically inclined, and Dietrich had many opportunities to learn and experiment with various instruments. He soon found his niche at the piano and on the violin, progressing rapidly toward mastery. Evening performances were part of the household routine. Dietrich refused to be left out. He often took the lead in organizing a Saturday evening of music for family and guests. He became an accomplished pianist at a young age. His musical gift included sight-reading. Because he could easily play music he had not seen before, Dietrich could accompany his sisters as they played cello and violin.[2]

Dietrich's first formal schooling outside of his home was at the Friedrich Werder Gymnasium, where he enrolled for the fall of 1913. His twin sister attended a different school, so for the first time Dietrich and Sabine were separated for much of their day. At first Dietrich was not fond of going to school. The route required crossing a large bridge, and he disliked doing it alone. But he adjusted and settled into a routine that still allowed him to spend evenings with his twin sister and their imaginative explorations.

The settled and secure existence of the Bonhoeffer family changed with the onset of World War I. Germany had a military alliance with Austria. When a Serbian student from Yugoslavia assassinated Austria's archduke Ferdinand, Austria responded by accusing the Serbian government. When Austria went to war against Yugoslavia, Germany honored its agreement and entered the conflict. This incident and the start of war in Europe gave Germany the opening it had been looking for. The emperor, Kaiser Wilhelm, had been making plans to invade other European countries for a long time. Now he put these plans in action, setting his eyes first on France.

The economy of Germany depended on trade with other countries. With the outbreak of war, many staples Germany needed stopped coming in, and the country plunged into a period of food shortage. Even families who could afford to buy food, such as the Bonhoeffers, had difficulty finding enough food to buy. Paula Bonhoeffer rallied with her usual indomitable spirit. Before long the family had a vegetable garden. Goats and poultry were a common sight in the yard. Paula was determined to improve the family's food supply. No one in the Bonhoeffer household—including the five servants who continued to serve the family despite difficult times—would go hungry. The economic plight of her country was another opportunity for Paula to put her organizational skills to work to benefit her family.[3]

Before long the war touched the family in a more direct way. The German kaiser roused the patriotism of the country as Germany's involvement in the war deepened. Two of Dietrich's brothers, Karl-Friedrich and Walter, were drafted to serve in the German army. The Bonhoeffers were a loyal family, who were proud to see their sons serve the Fatherland. Still, it was hard to send Karl-Friedrich and Walter off, not knowing what the future would bring. Dietrich was only eleven years old when Walter, still a teenager, faced his last night at home before beginning his army service. The youngest Bonhoeffer son put his musical talents to work and composed his own version of a song: "Now at the last, we say Godspeed on your journey." He sang his composition for Walter on the last evening they shared.[4]

The family followed the war closely. The German people began to lose faith in the conflict and wondered why they were sending their young men off to fight. Germany lost ground on the battlefront. Despite their early successes, it now seemed impossible to win. Too many other countries had entered the war and come to the defense of France, including Russia, England, and the United States. As young as Dietrich was, he had good reason to try to understand what was happening in his own country and around the world. Both of his brothers were wounded. Karl-Friedrich's wound healed quickly and he returned to his family. Walter was wounded a few months after joining the army and died during surgery in a field hospital five days after his injury. The innocence of Dietrich's privileged boyhood was over. Being a soldier to serve the Fatherland was no longer a patriotic dream. Walter was dead. Before he was a teenager himself, Dietrich saw his mother plunge into years of grief and depression following Walter's death.

Dietrich was fourteen when he made the life-changing decision to become a minister. His father, while not opposed to a profession in the church, was concerned that it would be too boring for his intellectual, sensitive son. Dietrich's brothers and sisters refused to take him seriously, scoffing at his choice and believing that he would abandon it before he was old enough to actually pursue it. They argued that the church was poor and uninteresting. Dietrich retorted that if those things proved true, then he would reform the church. Once during a Greek class, his teacher asked him what he planned to study at university. Dietrich's answer was "theology." The teacher responded, "Well, you are in for some surprises." But Dietrich didn't let such comments dissuade him. By the time he went through the classes and ceremony to be confirmed in the Lutheran Church at age fifteen, he was resolutely determined to become a minister and planned his future education with that goal in mind.

In 1923 Dietrich turned seventeen and was ready to enter the university. His family had a tradition of attending the university at Tubingen, and Dietrich followed this path. His childhood was over.

As Dietrich looked to his own future, his country struggled against the ravaging effects of World War I. The traditional monarchy had been destroyed. Wilhelm had fled, and his successor took the throne only long enough to sign a treaty to end the war—and the monarchy. Germany had no kaiser to lead the country. The terms of the treaty were a humiliation to German national pride. Leaders were forced to establish a new form of government in the republic of Germany. Dozens of small political parties sprang up and vied for dominance. Because of widespread poverty and unemployment, politicians who promised to make things better for everyone—not only the rich—gained popularity rapidly. This included the Communists and the Nazis. Aging leaders who had flourished under the monarchy now were frustrated to know how to lead the country. The German people, plunged into the economic after-effects of World War I and the global Depression, listened to one voice, then another, scrambling to find someone who might restore their national pride and comfortable, traditional way of life.

3

Higher Education

The first academic term in Tubingen was uneventful for Dietrich Bonhoeffer. Near the end of his second term, however, he had a skating accident. He was unconscious for a long period of time. The accident occurred around the time of his birthday, early in 1924, and was serious enough that Paula and Karl Bonhoeffer decided to travel from Berlin to visit their son. As he recovered, Dietrich talked about what he really wanted to do. He was not anxious to resume studies at Tubingen. Ultimately, he hoped to study theology in Berlin. This was the hub of leading German theological thinkers, and Dietrich wanted to be there. First, though, he wanted to travel. His parents agreed to a few months of studying outside of Germany, and Dietrich began making arrangements.

Dietrich traveled with his older brother Klaus. Their first stop was Rome. Dietrich found that he had little trouble picking up enough Italian to attend academic lectures and benefit from them. But what intrigued him most was his experience of the history of the Christian church. He spent long hours absorbing mosaics and other artistic renderings of the church and the Christian faith. He wandered the catacombs, where the Christians in the first century hid from their persecutors. There Dietrich pondered the brave choices Christians made to stand up against a government that made their lives more difficult by the day. He ventured outside of his Lutheran Church experience and worshiped in Catholic churches. He listened to the historic mass sung in Latin and thrived in the city that was the very center of the Roman Catholic Church. This visit to Rome gave the German Lutheran Dietrich Bonhoeffer an understanding that the Christian church was vaster and deeper than his experience of it up to that point. The Catholic Church, with its roots more than a thousand years older than his own Lutheran heritage, opened his eyes to the worldwide nature of the church.

After a brief visit to North Africa with Klaus, Dietrich returned to Berlin and entered the university there, the same university where his father was a professor. Here Dietrich began his serious theological studies. Because of his family background and his own superior ability as a student, his family expected that he would enter the professional world of theological studies after graduating from the university. He could easily pursue a career as a professor of theology and do very well. But Dietrich's real interest was in becoming a pastor, just as he had been saying ever since he was fourteen years old. Through the opportunities presented to him as a student, he found that he loved to preach. He preached his first public sermon on October 18, 1925, in Berlin. His mother was there to hear him expound on Luke 17:7–10. In this passage, Jesus teaches about faith and duty. A master gives direction to the servant, and the servant does his duty. Christianity means decision, change, and denial of the past, Dietrich said. Christians must be ready to answer the call of the Master, even if it means leaving everything behind.

The climax of Dietrich's career as a university student was writing a dissertation. He chose as his subject the "communion of saints." In his dissertation, Dietrich Bonhoeffer argued that all Christians are formed by their encounters with others. God made humans relational. We're meant to be in relationships with each other, and we're meant to be in relationship with God himself. Sometimes being in relation to other people means making a decision, a choice. We have an ethical responsibility to respond to others with whom we have relationships. A choice to do something that is good for someone else may mean self-sacrifice. Although just out of the university, Dietrich Bonhoeffer was formulating an approach to theology and ethics that would bear fruit in the decisions that he himself would face in the years to come. He was not interested in theoretical theology; he was interested in interpreting the Bible in a way that allows the Word to direct everyday choices.

During Dietrich's early university years, normal family life for the Bonhoeffers marched ahead. Several of his siblings married during these years. Ursula married Dr. Rudiger Schleicher in 1923. Christel married Hans von Dohnanyi, a talented lawyer, in 1925. And in 1926 Dietrich's twin, Sabine, married Gerhard Leibholz, a constitutional lawyer of Jewish origin. The family celebrated each occasion and welcomed these new members into their family. In the early and mid–1920s, no one could imagine how the choices of these spouses would influence the crises and responses that the Bonhoeffer family would face ten or fifteen years later.

Germany, the country that Dietrich loved, continued to try to get on solid footing economically and politically. War debt from World War I still weighed down the struggling nation. Inflation soared, prices rising literally every day. It took more than four trillion marks (the German currency) to equal one U.S. dollar. For many, a lifetime savings for retirement added up to enough money to buy a basket of strawberries. Political parties continued to promise prosperity if only they would be elected to the Reichstag, the German parliament. Germany had too many hungry and homeless people for the government to deal with. New parties, such as the Nazis, criticized the government for allowing the German people to suffer and promised improvement. With so many people poor and unemployed, this sort of political promise became very popular. People started to listen. One of the rising young political stars people watched was Adolf Hitler. During the mid–1920s, Adolf Hitler steadily climbed the ranks of the Nazi party at the same time that the party became more popular in the eyes of the German people.

Meanwhile, Dietrich continued to pursue his plan to become a pastor. In 1928 he passed an important set of theological exams. Now he needed practical experience in a pastorate. One month after his exams he left for Spain. His assignment was to serve as an assistant pastor to a German congregation in Barcelona. Dietrich was no longer in the world of academia. Now he faced a completely new challenge: ministering to ordinary people in the everyday moments of their lives. He had proven that he was a scholar. Now he would find out if he could be a pastor. His energy went into the practical tasks of the church that arose on a daily basis. One of his first assignments was to begin a Sunday school for children. On the first morning, one little girl came. But Dietrich was not deterred. He kept at it, and soon thirty children filled the room every week.[1]

The ministry in Barcelona put Dietrich in close contact with some very poor people in the neighborhood around the church. It didn't take long for Dietrich to face the reality that he was outside of his comfortable, financially secure world of a prestigious German family. He was face-to-face, shoulder-to-shoulder, with people who did not have enough to meet their basic needs. He saw people who were undernourished, homeless, jobless, oppressed, and desperate. Dietrich became convinced that the church had a responsibility to minister to the poor, and not just with sermons and kind words. The church should provide food to the hungry, clothing and medicine and jobs to those who needed them. For Dietrich, meeting basic needs was a fundamental way to show Christ to the world. How could the church—or individual Christians—do otherwise?

When his temporary assignment ended, the church leaders invited Dietrich to remain in Barcelona and continue the work he had begun. After serious thought, Dietrich decided to return to Berlin in 1929 and began working as a lecturer in systematic theology at the university. Holding this post required that he demonstrate an ability to handle the subject of his lectures in a way that brought credibility in an academic setting. He wrote *Act and Being* to satisfy this requirement, completing the scholarly work in February 1930. In this academic paper, Bonhoeffer spoke to philosophers and theologians who were too easily caught up in idealism and abstract ideas about the transcendence of God. True faith, he argued, is an experience of the concrete, present Christ who was made flesh, was crucified, and raised from the dead.[2]

In September 1930, as Dietrich planned his next professional step, Germany faced national elections. With several political parties active and growing, it was difficult for one party to gain a true majority of the popular vote. But the party with the largest number of representatives to the Reichstag would carry power and influence Germany's future. In the 1930 elections, the Nazi party gained seats in the Reichstag, becoming the second most powerful party in the country. Change stirred the German people, who hoped for a return to the prosperity and pride they had enjoyed before World War I.

In the wake of this election, Dietrich took advantage of an opportunity to study in the United States at Union Theological Seminary. He was a Sloane Fellow during this time, arriving at Union with several other foreign recipients of this scholarship. Dietrich was the German representative. Unlike other Sloane Fellows, he had already completed advanced-level theological studies. This meant he was free to study whatever interested him at Union rather than follow a structured program. For the most part he opted to study philosophy of religion.

America was in a crisis the year of Bonhoeffer's visit. The stock market had crashed the year before, plunging the country into economic depression that rebounded around the world. Almost immediately people who could not conceive of having extra money to invest in the stock market themselves were affected by its crash. Banks failed. Businesses closed their doors, letting employees go by the hundreds. There were no other jobs to be found. Unemployment soared. Poverty spread rapidly. Families who had been very poor, but getting by, now found themselves unable to put food on the table or keep a roof over their heads. Homelessness multiplied. No region of the country escaped the economic despair of the Depression. Whole segments of the population dropped several rungs on the economic ladder, including African-Americans in Harlem, not far from where Dietrich Bonhoeffer studied at Union Theological Seminary.

One of Dietrich's fellow students, Albert F. Fisher, was an African-American who moved freely in the streets of Harlem. Through this friendship, Bonhoeffer began attending the Abyssinian Baptist Church in the heart of Harlem, in New York City. The church was on a dreary, miserable street. Just getting there meant Dietrich had to walk through despairing neighborhoods full of people who had little hope: men without incomes, children and families living one day at a time, not knowing where supper would come from the next day. Dietrich saw the need and plunged in to do what he could to befriend the neighborhood around the church and minister to its people. He taught a Sunday school class for youth and a midweek Bible study for women. Occasionally he had an opportunity to preach. He fell in love with the gospel music of Harlem. He certainly had not heard this in his traditional German Lutheran Church! The entire experience was exhilarating and confusing at the same time. Dietrich felt stirrings inside himself that made him believe God was at work in Harlem—and in Dietrich Bonhoeffer.

Even more so than he did during the months in Barcelona, Dietrich saw needs in the lives of ordinary people. He asked himself over and over what the Christian's response should be. Not only did he witness economic suffering beyond what he had experienced in Germany, but he also saw racial prejudice at work. He became indignant about a society where the white population treated the black population with prejudice and hostility, yet called itself a Christian nation. How could this be? Dietrich wondered. And why did the American government not take action to correct such injustice?

While in New York, Dietrich wrote to a friend in Germany about his "new perspectives," which were affecting his views of philosophy and theology. Dietrich had gone to New York as a theologian. His experiences there turned him in the direction of exploring what it meant to be a Christian as well. He found himself turning away from academic theological language. The Bible was no longer simply sermon material. As he learned to read the Bible in a meditative way, he discovered that it was a practical guide to living the Christian life.

Dietrich's academic year at Union Theological Seminary came to an end, and he headed back to Europe. But his "new perspective" did not end. He carried it with him when he returned home. Many years later, writing from prison, Dietrich described this experience as his transition from "theologian" to "Christian."[3]

Before returning to Germany, however, he stopped in England for a conference in Cambridge. This was an ecumenical conference. Those who attended were interested in seeing churches of the world work together on issues that affected many countries, especially world peace. At this point, Dietrich did not have a serious interest in ecumenical issues. He was at heart a pastor, after all, not a conference speaker or social leader. Yet his experience of Harlem led him to think that Christians must respond to the injustice around them. While in the United States, Dietrich had come to know the World Alliance for Promoting International Friendship Through the Churches. When he was invited to attend their conference in Cambridge, he accepted. He made it clear from the start that his interest was in the practical issues of life, not strictly theology. How would the church respond to real issues that affected real people? At the conference, Dietrich was elected co-secretary for Germany and Central Europe, so his official link to the ecumenical movement began. The conference sent out a unanimous message to the churches of the world. War as a means of settling disputes between nations did not please Christ. Conference participants called for nations around the world to reduce their weaponry and work toward a reasonable and just relationship between nations.

Dietrich Bonhoeffer returned to Berlin in the summer of 1931 ready to continue lecturing in theology at the university while also taking an active part in church life, helping Christians to meet real needs.

4

Ministry to Youth

The Cambridge conference opened the door to more intense involvement for Dietrich in ecumenical circles. In the wake of World War I and in the midst of changing economic and political pressures, the ecumenical movement sought to motivate churches internationally. National leaders could not so easily ignore the combined voice of Christians around the world. The movement called for churches to speak up and be heard, especially on the issues of responding to injustice and striving for international relationships built on cooperation rather than war. Dietrich's overseas experience and his ability with foreign languages were an unusual combination. Adding his theological training to the mix put Dietrich in a class of his own. Leaders of the ecumenical movement were eager to have him participate. As long as he was allowed to work in the area of practical life issues, Dietrich was eager to be involved. In October 1931, shortly after his return to Berlin, he sent his first letters to organizations within his European area of responsibility. He was preparing for a major youth conference scheduled for the following year.

Still considering himself a pastor at heart, Dietrich
now pursued the path to formal ordination in the
German Lutheran Church. This became a third focal
point of his life, after his lecturing responsibilities and
his ecumenical work. His superiors in the church
assigned him to a confirmation class in the Zion Parish
of Berlin. Dietrich happily took on this responsibility,
looking forward to working with the youth. The class
proved to be more of a challenge than he anticipated.

The confirmation class of fifty children was out of
control. The older minister running the class was at
the end of his rope. The class had a will of its own, and
none of the students was learning anything about the
Christian faith. Nothing the minister tried caused the
children to behave in the manner he thought appropri-
ate. He was more than willing to introduce a young
man still in his twenties to this rambunctious crowd.
With Dietrich right behind him, the older man barely
managed to get into the classroom and shout an introduction of Dietrich, which none of the students listened
to. They were too busy running wild in the classroom
and the hallway and the stairs. As soon as the required
introduction was complete, the man left. Apparently
now that Dietrich had been assigned to teach the class,
he felt no more responsibility to deal with the unruly
crowd.

Dietrich put his hands in his pockets and leaned
against the wall of the classroom. He did not speak at
first, and made no attempt to subdue the young people.
He shouted no instructions, gave no commands, made
no movement to physically control the students.
Minutes passed, and still Dietrich stood with his hands
in his pockets, leaning against the wall, saying nothing. Finally his failure to react to the bedlam made
an impression. If the students could not upset the
new teacher with their behavior, what was the point of

continuing? Some of the children began to control themselves and turn their attention to Dietrich, perhaps out of curiosity more than anything else. In response, he began to speak very quietly and calmly. Only those who were immediately before him in the front row could hear what he said. His strategy paid off. In only a matter of minutes the class was silent. Dietrich was telling a story of his work in Harlem, in the United States. The German youngsters were curious about faraway America and began to listen. Dietrich had them in the palm of his hand. He promised them more stories of Harlem if they would behave and listen to him. He never had a moment's trouble again.[1]

Dietrich took his work with the confirmation students seriously. He did not just teach a class once a week, and he did not withdraw every evening to the comfort of his parents' well-appointed home. He lived in the neighborhood where his students lived. He saw the daily rigors of their families. He witnessed the indescribable poverty that was all they had ever known, the lack of food and basic shelter. He saw the immorality that surrounded them and gave them their skewed values. Yet even in these circumstances Dietrich reached his students and found them open to the Christian faith. He had the academic credentials to be gainfully employed in the academic world of theology. If he had so chosen, Dietrich Bonhoeffer would never have had to walk through the streets of the poverty-stricken parts of Berlin. He could have lived in a comfortable home, enjoyed rich, nourishing meals, and spent his time debating the finer points of theology. He would never have had to be anywhere near the filth and immorality that his students knew on a daily basis. But Dietrich had not forgotten Barcelona. He had not forgotten Harlem. He had not forgotten the ecumenical movement's call for the church to respond to injustice. Dietrich Bonhoeffer was in touch with real life and took the call to respond seriously.

The confirmation class followed its course and came to an end. But Dietrich was not ready to walk away from the needs of youth. He opened a Youth Club in Berlin in the summer of 1932. And he pursued his role in the upcoming Youth Conference in Czechoslovakia with a fresh passion. The conference was held in August 1932. Dietrich had done his job in helping to organize it, and it was in good order. But during the conference, a new role emerged for which Dietrich was uniquely suited. Dietrich saw that the ecumenical movement needed more than good organizers. It needed more than well-attended conferences. It needed more than a current cause to rally around. The move- ment needed theological roots. The belief that the church ought to respond to social injustices, in Die- trich's mind, must be rooted in an understanding of the very nature of the church. He came to believe that if the ecumenical movement did not produce its own the- ology to steer its future, it would become just another reorganization of one conference after another. In the past Dietrich had said he wanted to be involved in the movement to work on real-life issues. Now he saw that the very work he committed himself to needed a theo- logical foundation to carry it into the future. Confer- ences to say what ought to be done would never be enough. Pronouncements and general principles must never take the place of action.

Bonhoeffer began asking some key questions that the ecumenical movement would face in the next dec- ade: With what authority does the church speak when it declares the claims of Christ to the world? *The church must look to the Bible to know what to proclaim to the world*. In attempting to answer these questions in his own mind, Dietrich began a lifelong study of the

Sermon on the Mount. This brief passage of Scripture charted his course theologically and practically when he faced choices that made him take theology out of the academic realm and into real life. His new personal commitment to devotional reading of the Bible began to show. Students, friends, and family saw that he had come home from New York a changed man. He formed deep habits of prayer and Bible reading. Some who had known him for years wondered if he had become fanatical. Reflecting on his discovery of the power of the Bible and a personal relationship with Jesus, Dietrich later wrote that he had often preached about the church, but he had not yet become a Christian. Now he had. While he did not dwell on the details of his conversion in a public way, he had no reservations about its impact on his life and work. Clearly it changed his perspectives on what it meant to be both a theologian and a pastor.[2]

Dietrich Bonhoeffer was first committed to his own church, the German Lutheran tradition that was born in his own country in the days of Martin Luther. He never ceased to find inspiration in the writings of Martin Luther and quoted the great reformer often in his own writings. Dietrich was next committed to the ecumenical movement. He was first drawn to the movement because he was a firm pacifist, convinced that violence never settled anything. Mohandas Gandhi, the renowned Indian pacifist, was a personal hero. Several times Dietrich made plans to travel to India and meet Gandhi in person. Each time personal commitments prevented him from making the trip. Nevertheless, Gandhi influenced Bonhoeffer deeply. As he got involved in the ecumenical movement, Dietrich became more and more convinced that peace was only possible if the church around the world united in its efforts to avert war.

After the youth conference in August, two elections in ecumenical circles occurred that impacted Dietrich's life. First, Bishop George Bell of Chichester, England, became president of the ecumenical council. Second, Karl Barth, a German theologian whom Dietrich admired, was elected to the theological committee of life and work. Dietrich's personal relationships with both Bell and Barth were just beginning. But in only a matter of months Dietrich's life would take a course from which there would be no turning back.

The same international tensions and economic crises that prompted the compassionate hearts of the ecumenical movement to action also fueled political juggling. Just days before the opening of the ecumenical conference that Dietrich helped plan, elections in Germany gave the Nazis even more seats in the Reichstag. Although they did not have a majority of the country's vote, they gained enough seats to become the most powerful political party. Now they increased pressure on the president of Germany, Hindenburg, to appoint a chancellor from within the Nazi party. The German chancellor would be second in command, accountable to the president. Adolf Hitler was the rising star of the Nazi party. Hindenburg came from a traditional, conservative political background. He had been a field marshal in World War I and had served under Germany's monarchy. He considered the Nazis too modern and radical and hesitated to give them too much power. A Nazi chancellor would make his job as president more complicated, particularly one with as strong and demanding a personality as Adolf Hitler's. President Hindenburg turned to other candidates for the chancellor position. Although they were experienced politicians, these men turned out to be weak leaders once in the chancellor role. Hitler's popularity was on the rise, and he pressed again to be made chancellor.

In late November 1932, a group of prominent, powerful businessmen signed a letter asking Hindenburg to appoint Adolf Hitler as chancellor of Germany. Hindenburg was an old man by now and tired of fighting. He gave in and made Hitler chancellor.

5

The Rise of German Dictatorship

On January 30, 1933, the news broke out that Hindenburg had named Hitler chancellor of Germany. Hitler had been a growing political nuisance for years. Although the Nazi party did not have a majority of popular votes, they now held the seat of power. Many German intellectual leaders had thought that a man with the extreme views Hitler held would never be taken seriously. Certainly the intellectual circles of Germany, in which Dietrich Bonhoeffer lived, thought that Hitler could come to nothing. But they were wrong; the day had come.

Hitler had come to his position of power in exactly the way the German constitution prescribed. His cabinet, at first, included people from a conglomeration of political parties, only one of which was the National Socialist German Workers' Party, known as the Nazis. Hitler immediately began talking about a "national awakening." The fourteen years since the end of World War I and Germany's humiliation represented a shameful past. Hitler wanted to awaken and reconstruct Germany into a powerful nation.[1]

Though his rise to power was strictly legal, Hitler did make special demands when he became chancellor. He wanted much more independent power than chancellors before him had. President Hindenburg had to promise not to get in Hitler's way. Hitler also demanded new elections for a new government, hoping to fill the Reichstag with Nazi representatives.

The news of Hitler's rise to power caused alarm in the Bonhoeffer home. No one tried to hide the concern they all shared. Hans von Dohnanyi, husband of Dietrich's older sister Christel, worked in the Ministry of Justice and warned the family that their lives would be turned inside out very quickly. But even with the warning, no one in the family realized how swift and drastic the changes would be.

Just two days later, twenty-seven-year-old Dietrich saw for himself how speedily life was altered for them all. Dietrich was scheduled to give a talk on the radio. His title was "The Leader and the Individual in the Younger Generation." Just how Dietrich came to be behind a radio microphone only two days after Hitler declared himself "Fuhrer" is not clear, except that the radio talk might have been arranged by the university. Dietrich's father had made a broadcast a few weeks earlier about mental illness, which had been arranged by the university. Dietrich's talk might also have been on behalf of the Student Christian Movement. In any event, he was prepared for the talk and presented himself at the radio station as planned. Although the talk had been scheduled before Hitler's rise, now Dietrich's subject was sure to bring consternation, for he was ready to argue that a Fuhrer, a leader, can quickly become a Verfuhrer, a misleader, if young people persisted in making idols of their leaders. A "misleader" who sets himself up as a god mocks the true God, Dietrich argued. He began his talk, following his manuscript closely. Suddenly someone switched off the microphone just as Dietrich came to the climax of his talk. He was about to make his point about false leaders. Because of the subject matter and the timing of his talk, it seems unlikely that he simply ran out of time. Someone had found his talk objectionable enough to stop it. But Dietrich would not be stopped. He had a complete script of his talk, well thought out and carefully worded. It was no great effort to duplicate the manuscript and send it to friends and colleagues. Before long the complete text of the talk was printed in a newspaper, and Dietrich was invited to give a longer version of it as a lecture at Berlin's College of Political Science. So at the age of twenty-seven, Dietrich Bonhoeffer was thrust to the forefront of church groups and political discussion. His quiet, private existence quickly turned into a public life under the scrutiny of Hitler's political machinery.

Within two days of Hitler's rise to power, the Nazis began a program to censor letters and listen in on telephone conversations. They burned books at the university and put pressure on professors to change their curriculum so that students would learn what the Nazis wanted them to learn. In a February 1, 1933, proclamation, Hitler promised that his government would "firmly protect Christianity, which is our moral basis." He concluded his talk that day by asking for God's mercy and guidance on his work.[2] Privately, though, many suspected that Hitler was looking for any reason he could find to clamp down on the independence of the Christian church. Hitler wanted no group, private or public, to operate outside of his scope of authority.

President Hindenburg had promised new elections, and now he set the date for March 5. All the parties went into action with their propaganda and campaigns.

This was a fresh opportunity to influence the vote and gain power in the Reichstag. Dramatically, one week before the elections, the Reichstag building, the center of German government, went up in a blaze. Hitler went to Hindenburg with a document he had conveniently prepared in advance. It was an emergency decree "for the protection of the people and the state." Publicly Hitler blamed the fire on a conspiracy of Jews and Communists, both groups whom he detested. The fact that Hitler had already prepared a document for the president to sign gave rise to other theories about how the fire started. Nothing was ever proven. Regardless of how the fire started, the event stirred up political tensions that could harm the country. Hindenburg signed the emergency decree.

Under a state of emergency, Hitler could make sweeping and immediate changes in the legal system. He drastically restricted personal liberties, claiming that it was for the good of the country. Hitler also instituted a "treachery law" that allowed the arrest of anyone who might spread an opinion contrary to the government. Newspapers were no longer free to print whatever they wanted. New laws prohibited people from assembling in public places. The government took over the mail, the telegraph, and the telephone systems so that private communication by these methods was virtually impossible. The Gestapo, the secret state police of the Nazi regime, could search any house and confiscate anything they wanted from private property. The state of emergency gave complete control to Hitler, doing away with almost all personal rights for the German people and making concentration camps possible.[3]

The March 5 elections occurred just as Hitler planned. When they were over, the Nazi party had control of the Reichstag with barely 36 percent of the people's vote. Hitler did not lift the emergency decree as most people had expected he would. In fact, he openly abandoned the constitution and legal system of Germany. For years the country remained under a perpetual state of emergency that gave enormous powers to one man—Adolf Hitler.

Hitler wasted no time making radical changes. On March 12 he declared that the swastika, the symbol of the Nazi party, would fly alongside the German flag. On April 1 he issued a one-day boycott of all Jewish businesses. Signs all around the country accused anyone who made a purchase in a shop run by Jews of being a traitor. Less than a week later, Hitler removed anyone of Jewish heritage from the civil service in Germany. Overnight people with Jewish ancestry were no longer qualified to serve their country in these jobs. This was the first of hundreds of laws that systematically excluded German Jews from businesses, professions, athletics, even going to public beaches or ski slopes. Almost immediately, the Nazis began acting on an Aryan policy that removed non-Aryans from their jobs in any official capacity. Important positions were only for Germans who had a pure German background. This was Hitler's way of expressing his hatred for the Jews. Anyone with even a partial Jewish background could no longer work in a government position or a civil service job. It didn't matter if a person's family had been in Germany for generations or the person had served nobly in the German government or the military. Jews were out. By the middle of July, Hitler declared that the Nazi party was the only legal political party in Germany. Anyone who tried to organize another party would face criminal charges.[4] In less than six months Germany became a nation that many of its citizens barely recognized.

Despite Hitler's early assurances that he would

"protect" Christianity, very early on people like Dietrich Bonhoeffer recognized that Nazism was an enemy of Christianity. Perhaps Hitler intended to deceive the German people about his feelings about the church to gain their allegiance and infiltrate the church hierarchy. In any event, it was not long before the established church became a target for his persecution. Christian teaching affirms that individual conscience and obedience to God come before allegiance to man. Hitler could not tolerate this way of thinking and still achieve the total control he demanded.

The Bonhoeffers and others in their circle of academic friends were appalled. Dietrich soon experienced another brush with the rising Nazi power. His Youth Club in Berlin was immediately suspect in the eyes of the Nazi party. Fellow workers at the Youth Club were forced out. Some of the members were known to be Communists, and they were openly harassed in the streets. The police searched the premises of the club, hoping to find a list of members to help them flush out more Communists. Dietrich resisted at first. The club had only been open a few months. But police interference made their work difficult and risky. Organizers of the club soon reconciled to closing down.

In this hostile climate, Dietrich's twin sister experienced the death of her Jewish father-in-law, who had never been baptized into the Christian church. Sabine and her husband, Gerhard, asked Dietrich to perform the funeral service. He deeply wanted to respond to his sister's request, but he was persuaded to consult with his ministerial superiors, and their advice was that he not conduct a funeral for a Jew at this particular point in time. Dietrich declined to participate.

The Nazis took over every part of German life, including the Christian church. The "German Christians" became the voice of the Nazi Party within religious circles. They began a campaign to place members of the party in key elected church positions. They wanted all ministers to produce evidence that they were not of Jewish descent. The Nazi infiltration was effective right from the start. Christians in Germany in 1933 were a mixed group without strong theological roots. Some found it easy to say that Martin Luther himself had marked the rise of German people in the Christian world, and that Germany was destined by God to be a leader of the Christian church. In order to be the leader, the church needed to be pure. Two factions of the church strained against each other: those whose emphasis was on their German identity and those whose focus was on their Christian identity.

In the summer of 1933, the "German Christians" influenced by the Nazis proposed the Aryan Paragraph. This was an official church policy that would prevent anyone who was not of Aryan descent from becoming a Christian minister or a teacher of religion. Whether the person was a believing Christian did not matter. What did matter was that the person was of pure Aryan descent. This policy would exclude Christians who had some Jewish background. Jews could no longer even become a member of the Christian church through the ceremony of baptism.

Most of the German bishops at the time wanted to avoid antagonizing the Nazis and did not consider the Aryan Paragraph an issue over which to fight. Dietrich Bonhoeffer revolted against this policy immediately, arguing fiercely that such a policy would surrender the heart of the Christian gospel to a political agenda. He responded by writing an essay on the Jewish question that cut to the heart of the issue: the church must decide how it would respond to the government's actions against the Jews. Bonhoeffer argued that the church had an obligation to fight injustice. For several years his academic thought had been meeting his personal experience as he confronted poverty and injustice in Barcelona, Harlem, and the heart of Berlin. When faced with the big questions, Dietrich did not back down. He argued three phases of the church's responsibility:

1. The church must ask whether the action the government has taken is a legitimate one. Can it be justified?
2. Next, the church must actively work to help the victims of the state's actions. On this point Dietrich was not talking only about Christians in the church but anyone in German society who was a victim of the state's actions. Surely he had the Jews in mind in particular.
3. Last, if the state is misusing the law and its own power, the church must step in. It's not good enough simply to bind up the wounds of the victims beneath the wheel. The church must do something to stop the wheel from turning and crushing more victims.[5]

Dietrich knew what he was saying when he put these words on paper. He knew the risk he was taking personally. Whether inside or outside the church, Nazi leaders would not like what he had to say. His own thinking clarified, Dietrich regretted that he had not performed the funeral for Sabine's father-in-law. He wrote to her later in the year expressing his deep remorse over the decision that he had made in April. His letter expressed the torment he experienced because he did not do as she had asked him to do. From the perspective of a few months later, he could not imagine what had made him behave the way he did. Sabine had accepted his decision without judgment, but Dietrich asked for forgiveness and said clearly that he ought to have behaved differently.[6]

During the summer, Dietrich worked hard to influence upcoming church elections. He even canceled his lectures at the university for the entire week of the elections and enlisted his students in the night-and-day task of election preparations. He wrote and duplicated leaflets to influence people not to vote for the Nazi candidates. The Gestapo confiscated his leaflets. Dietrich drove straight to the Gestapo headquarters and reminded the officials that the state had promised that the church elections would be free and fair. The Gestapo officials agreed to return the leaflets on the condition that Dietrich change some of his wording so that the German Christians who supported the Nazis did not look so negative. By this point in time, it was too late for new literature to have any impact. In the end, the church elections were overwhelmingly in favor of the Nazi candidates. Key German Christians, handpicked by Hitler, moved into key church positions.

Shortly after the elections, Dietrich preached a sermon that declared that nothing would be easy. Christians were confronted by a decision that would mean a parting of the ways. He called his listeners to journey with him back to the Holy Scriptures and look for the church together. The church must remain the church and "confess, confess, confess."[7]

Confess what? Dietrich was prepared to help answer this question. Shortly after this sermon, he became part of a small group of people sent off to a retreat site to write a first draft of a "Confession." Christians in Germany who wanted to set themselves apart from the Nazi-influenced German Christians in traditional churches could band together and stand by this Confession. This was the very first step toward a separate church structure in Germany, one that was not dominated by Nazi leaders. By August Bonhoeffer was firmly entrenched in his conviction that he could not belong to a church that excluded Jews. His views isolated him more and more from the circle of friends who were not willing to go as far out on a limb as Dietrich Bonhoeffer was.

In the fall Dietrich received an invitation to pastor a church in Berlin. He considered himself a pastor, and based on exterior circumstances, many thought he would be pleased to pastor a church in his own city. But Dietrich turned down the offer. His non-Aryan colleagues would not even be allowed to apply for the open pastorate, and he could not bring himself to accept a position in a church that would discriminate against a minister with Jewish origins. He wrote to his theologian friend Karl Barth that "it was time to go for a while into the desert."

Instead of pastoring in Berlin, Dietrich accepted an invitation from George Bell in England to pastor two German congregations in London. Was Dietrich running away from the trouble in Germany? Some might have thought so, including Karl Barth, who did not understand Dietrich's decision. But Dietrich did not see it that way. He had become frustrated with the cowardly position of the church in Germany. The time had come to look beyond the German church to the worldwide church. Dietrich knew that if he went to England, he could expand his international ecumenical contacts. He could begin by pleading with the English churches to put pressure on their government to intervene in Germany. He would be a voice for those who had no voice: the Jews. In England he could tell people face-to-face about the resistance of some believers to the direction the official German church was taking.

Perhaps the most surprising part of Hitler's rise was that most Germans seemed to accept this new state with nearly no resistance. Hitler's regime brought radical change to Germany. In the eyes of the world, his leadership made it more difficult to hold peaceful discussions. By October 1933 Germany withdrew from the League of Nations, which had been established at the end of World War I to promote world peace and cooperation. Clearly the country was separating itself from the goodwill of the world. Yet by November more than 95 percent of the German people approved of Hitler's leadership.

6

The German Church in London

D ietrich Bonhoeffer settled into London to pastor two small German congregations. His mother, as usual, made sure that he was well looked after. She provided a housekeeper and sent him furniture, even a grand piano so he could continue his music. In addition to his pastoral work in London, Dietrich's primary concern was the connections he could make for ecumenical work. In particular, he deepened his relationship with George Bell, the Bishop of Chichester, who had recognized Dietrich's value to the ecumenical movement and influenced his decision to come to London. George Bell became one of Dietrich's closest friends.

In London, Dietrich's churches quickly became havens for German Christian refugees. Many had Jewish backgrounds and had made the painful decision to leave their homeland because of the persecution they experienced in Germany. Dietrich's personal relationships with people like this fueled his determination to do something meaningful to help them. He became even more firmly convinced that Christians must stand

up against the Nazi take-over of the Christian church.
He continued to stir up resistance both in Germany,
from a distance, and in England through his day-to-day
work.

Dietrich stayed closely connected to others still in
Germany who agreed with him. While many Christian
leaders in Germany were willing to go along with what
the Nazis wanted in order to avoid confrontation, Dietrich found others who were willing to stand up against
what they believed was wrong.

In May 1934 leaders of this resistance group gathered in Barmen, Germany, and formally organized the
"Confessing Church." They were anxious to set themselves apart from the "German Christians" in mainstream churches. Ever since the days of Luther in the
sixteenth century, Christians in Germany had enjoyed
a solid, unified identity in the Lutheran Church that
had sprung from their own soil. Now Dietrich and the
others found themselves taking the same bold step
Martin Luther had taken when he called for Christians
to stand up against the injustices and misguided theological interpretations that Luther found in the Catholic Church of his own day. This was their turn to invoke
the wrath of both the government and the established
church because they believed they were acting on biblical grounds. Luther had fought the battle with the
belief that justification came by faith alone—people
became Christians through faith in Christ, not by anything that they could do for themselves. Dietrich Bonhoeffer now lifted the same banner: God's Word has not
changed. All who come to God through faith in Christ
are true believers, true Christians, regardless of
national or ethnic heritage. He simply could not stand
on the sidelines and watch churches give up this basic
tenet of the Christian faith.

"The Confessing Church" became the term that set

apart those who did not want to be associated with the German Christians and the anti-Jewish practices. All around Germany pockets of Christians believed as Dietrich Bonhoeffer did. Many were influenced or persuaded by his writings. At the end of May they came together for their first national gathering.

With the others in Barmen in 1934, Dietrich helped to form the Confessing Church fully aware that this action would cut them off from Hitler's so-called protection. Participating in the Barmen Confession also would isolate Dietrich from lifelong friends who did not share his view on this issue. The Confessing Church would have to start all over again with basic structures, such as a school for training its pastors, because they would not be welcome in the Nazi-infiltrated universities and seminaries that already existed. Anyone joining the Confessing Church would never be allowed to hold a position or minister to a congregation in the official German Christian Church. The German government was sure to scrutinize this fragment of the church and probably look for reasons to interfere with what the Confessing Church hoped to accomplish. Despite the weight of all these sacrifices, the "Barmen Confession," which Dietrich helped to write, became the cornerstone of the new movement of Christians within Germany.

The Barmen Confession argued against the false teaching that its writers believed had influenced the German churches. They hung their argument on 1 Corinthians 1:30: "It is because of him that you are in Christ Jesus. . . ." They also cited John 14:6: "I am the way and the truth and the life. No one comes to the Father except through me." Salvation comes only through Christ. The Barmen Confession rejected any authority other than the Word of God. The church cannot recognize other powers or personalities as divine truth, only Christ. While the German Christians were willing to play along with the Nazis, the Confessing Church came off the fence and made its position clear to the world. Still they faced an uphill battle for recognition and existence.

Life in Germany spiraled toward terror. At the end of June, about a month after the Barmen Confession, a large group within the Nazi Party attempted a rebellion against Hitler, their own leader. But Hitler was prepared. On the morning of June 30, death squads fanned out through Berlin. Truckloads of Nazi soldiers roamed the streets. Anyone suspected of being involved with a revolt against Hitler was shot on sight. Hitler himself went to the place where the leader of the revolt was sleeping and shot him in his bed. Hitler used this opportunity to remove anyone who opposed him, including a number of conservative leaders who were not part of the Nazi Party. It seemed that he wanted to teach a lesson to anyone who was thinking about opposing him. More than two hundred people died that day. At first the public was horrified. But the Nazis launched a public relations campaign to calm public opinion. People came to believe that the terror and violence was just the Nazis sowing the last of their wild oats. Hitler could still be trusted to lead the country back to prosperity and power.[1]

At the beginning of August, the aged President Hindenburg died of natural causes at his home. With him died the last hope that anyone could influence Hitler to be less severe in his policies. By noon on the day of Hindenburg's death, Hitler announced a new law. He claimed that government leaders had approved this one day earlier. Under the new law, the offices of president and chancellor were combined. Hitler was now the single leader of Germany, accountable to no one. And because the country was still in a "state of emergency," the rule of law was exchanged for the whims of Hitler.

Nevertheless, Hitler's popularity among the German people continued to rise. His regime had brought economic success. Despite his assurances that he did not want war, he was preparing a strong army. Along with clever finances and trade policies, this contributed to the recovery that Germany's economy needed. Mass unemployment was becoming a thing of the past. Agriculture thrived once again. Industry and manufacturing flourished. The standard of living for the Aryan population was on the rise, so many people in Germany were pleased with Hitler's leadership.[2] The effect on the daily lives of a struggling population was positive. Not everyone looked at the larger picture of political principles or international relations.

Bonhoeffer and others looked beyond the economic progress and promises of prosperity to the underlying mentality of Nazi leaders. They saw the danger that Hitler was to the church and invoked a higher allegiance to Christ. Bonhoeffer dared to step out of the mainstream, isolate himself from his friends, and risk his professional career because he believed that Hitler was dangerous not only to society but also to the church. All of his early ethical thinking about being in relationship to others and making difficult choices burst into reality as he faced those choices himself. Helping to found the Confessing Church was such a choice.

A partial test of the Confessing Church's success came only a few weeks after the Barmen Confession and in the wake of the June 30 massacre. Ecumenical groups from around the world met at the World Alliance in Denmark. The Confessing Church could muster no delegates from within Germany. The established German Christians controlled the appointment of

German delegates. Clearly they would not appoint anyone from the Confessing Church to represent the Christians of Germany in an ecumenical, international gathering. Against this backdrop, Dietrich Bonhoeffer was asked to speak at the conference in Denmark. He spoke passionately to the international gathering that peace comes by a road that leads to the cross, directing the entire assembly to the fundamentals of the Christian faith. He held high the banner that the ecumenical efforts toward world peace must have a theological grounding in the cross of Christ. Dietrich's talk was received with overwhelming acceptance and pushed him even further toward the forefront of ecumenical work. But perhaps more significant is the fact that he was recognized at that assembly as a representative of the Confessing Church. By this act, Dietrich Bonhoeffer helped to establish recognition from around the world for the Confessing Church alongside the German Christians.

Dietrich returned to London to lead his congregations to formally withdraw from the official German church before the end of the year. The Confessing Church, while still in its infancy, was standing on its own two feet before the world.

7

The Founding of Finkenwalde Seminary

The Nazi government left no stone unturned, including the educational system of Germany. Children in the early grades of school learned the Nazi way of thinking. Private schools that resisted were pressured out of existence. Under the state of emergency, Nazis ruthlessly took over places of higher learning, pushing out of the universities anyone who would not modify curriculum to support the Nazi agenda. They clamped down on free-thinking intellectual individuals. The only acceptable way to think was the Nazi way, and anyone who resisted could expect trouble. Being Aryan was no longer good enough; only Nazi-sympathizers could hope to hold positions of prestige or influence.

With the birth of the Confessing Church in this context, it would obviously need its own system for training future leaders. And if the Confessing Church were to be credible in the eyes of the world, it needed a seminary. Leaders of the Confessing Church called upon Dietrich Bonhoeffer, and in March 1935 he returned from London to Germany to establish a brand-new seminary for students of the Confessing Church. The decision was not an easy one for Bonhoeffer: he had a flourishing ministry among Germans in England, a thriving friendship with George Bell, and ongoing opportunities to influence the ecumenical movement work so that it would benefit Germany in the eyes of the world. But in his heart, Dietrich wrestled with the crisis of the church in Germany. He could not have stayed in London, secure and safe, knowing that his countrymen and fellow believers faced persecution and turmoil at home. He believed that the church should do more than preach peace. The church must stand up for those deprived of their rights. And how could he preach this theme unless he also lived it? So he went home to found and lead the seminary. Dietrich Bonhoeffer became an employee of the Old Prussian Council of Brethren, one of the church groups participating in the Confessing Church movement. Although he was later on leave, technically he remained an employee of the Old Prussian Council of Brethren for the rest of his life.

The Confessing Church found space for a seminary in Finkenwalde, a countryside community north of Berlin. The property had once been part of a large estate in a small country town. The main building had most recently been used as a school, which had been closed down by the Nazis. It was up to Dietrich and his students to furnish the buildings. The early weeks of the seminary featured a great deal of improvisation and "make-do" mindset. Dietrich's own work habits were remarkable. He managed to do in a couple of hours what others would need a whole day to accomplish. Sometimes this made him unsympathetic to others who struggled to keep up with the pace he set.[1] But Dietrich Bonhoeffer pressed on. He lobbied for donations of money, food, furniture, and books from Confessing Church congregations throughout Germany. He

urged people to give what was needed both to start up
the seminary and to keep it going on a monthly basis.
Eventually they acquired two grand pianos for a music
room and used whitewash, packing cases, and coarse
cotton cloth to create a chapel out of a room that had
once served as a gymnasium. Dietrich Bonhoeffer's
personal collection of theological books formed the
backbone of the seminary library.[2]

The location of the seminary in Pomerania, a rural
region away from major cities, took Dietrich Bonhoeffer out of the familiar urban academic world and into a
new way of life. Many of the students of the seminary,
like Dietrich, came from homes and families where
they had all they needed and wanted: servants made
sure things ran smoothly. Spacious structures gave
everyone the room they needed to live comfortably and
even entertain from time to time. Coming from such a
background, Finkenwalde was a shock. Here they slept
all in one large room and kept few personal belongings.
Furnishings were minimal, food unpredictable, and
privacy unheard of. But they came in answer to the call
for future leaders of the Confessing Church.

Perhaps the biggest surprise of Finkenwalde was
Dietrich Bonhoeffer's vision for a community of faith
that shared life in intentional structured ways. The
courses the seminary offered were usual for a school
preparing preachers: homiletics, pastoral care, liturgi-
cal studies. But one theme that set Finkenwalde apart
was Bonhoeffer's passion for discipleship. His teaching
was dominated by a series of lectures on discipleship—
and the insistence that students live out the meaning
of discipleship.[3] Dietrich was not concerned only for the
intellectual or academic development of his students.
He was deeply interested in the formation of their spiritual disciplines, and he worked hard to accomplish
this at Finkenwalde. His expectations were clear but

high. A strict regimen began early in the morning with thirty minutes of silent meditation on one biblical text. Dietrich chose a portion of the Bible from Martin Luther's own translation and assigned students to meditate on the same brief portion every morning for an entire week. Then the student body gathered for a morning service around a large dinner table. They sang the psalm for the day and the hymn for the day, heard the Scripture readings assigned to that day, and prayed together. When the academic portion of the day began, it was no less stringent. Dietrich himself did the teaching, giving lectures and assigning written work. The day ended with another worship service around the table. On Saturdays Dietrich included a sermon.

Dietrich also began the practice of individual confession of sin. Each student could choose one other person to whom he would be accountable. Dietrich led by example and did not require anything of his students that he was not also deeply involved in, whether it was confession or meditation or worship. If the weather was particularly fine, Dietrich might spontaneously cancel classes and take students for a hike in the woods. He did not allow anyone to do academic work on Sundays. Instead, he filled the day with games and experiences everyone could share. One evening each week was set aside for students to discuss current events. Dietrich did not want his students to undergo a theological education that was not intimately connected with life in the world around them. Their time at Finkenwalde was to prepare them both spiritually and academically to interact with the political and economic events swirling around them in Germany.

Some students and supporters began to think the seminary was too much like a monastery and not enough like a school. But Dietrich believed in the expression of faith through relationships. The call that had brought them all to Finkenwalde in the first place ought to continue to bind them together as they lived each day sharing resources and experiences. Some students considered him quite eccentric, but Dietrich did not tolerate anyone trying to escape the regimen. To be a part of Finkenwalde meant not only being a student but also living life together.

Two of Dietrich Bonhoeffer's most influential writings came out of this period of time: *Life Together* and *The Cost of Discipleship*. In both books he wrote about the transforming nature of true faith. Truly becoming a disciple of Jesus Christ radically changes an individual's life. Simply agreeing with the teaching of the church is not enough. In the faith community that he formed at Finkenwalde, Dietrich was looking for a concrete experience of the body of Christ. His underlying convictions about the social nature of the Christian church had been formed during his university days. Now he had the opportunity to see the church as a social organization. Jesus calls individuals, Bonhoeffer believed, not so they can disappear in the crowd, but so that believers are connected through their experience of faith and self-sacrificing discipleship. From this experience of living out the experiment came the two books for which Bonhoeffer is most famous.

The Cost of Discipleship is Bonhoeffer's most famous work. While running the seminary at Finkenwalde, Bonhoeffer began to articulate the principles and convictions that undergirded the community. After his own experience of conversion during his time in New York, Dietrich was convinced that the true Christian would be transformed by an encounter with Christ. In his teachings and writings, especially in *The Cost of Discipleship*, Bonhoeffer talked about the difference between "lukewarm" Christians and true disciples of Christ. The true disciple is devoted to Christ and willing to pay whatever price is necessary to follow Him. The grace of God came at a price—the price of His own Son's life. Believers should not cheapen God's grace by thinking that they have no price to pay. Christ's death provides the way of salvation. The Christian must rise and follow Christ, being willing to be transformed by Christ, and even to suffer for the cause of Christ. At Finkenwalde, Bonhoeffer pressed his students to open themselves up to the transformation that Christ could bring to them. (See Appendix 3 for more on Bonhoeffer's writings.)

In September Dietrich was called away from his teaching to a gathering of Confessing Church leaders in Steglitz, a suburb of Berlin. Yet another time of reckoning had come to the young Confessing Church. At the Steglitz conference, they wrestled with several issues. First, the Nazi regime had made laws that gave it increasing power in church issues, primarily by controlling the financial affairs of local congregations. Church leaders wrestled with how important it might be to resist government control over church finances.[4] These regulations applied to all churches, whether Catholic, German Christian, or Confessing Church congregations. Some within the Confessing Church argued that it was not an issue worth antagonizing the Nazis over. Others saw it as one more step toward squelching the voice of Christians once and for all.

The Steglitz conference came on the heels of the Nuremberg laws. Named for the city where they were announced, the Nuremberg laws were short and to the point. Jews were no longer full German citizens, and a non-Jew could not legally marry a Jew. The Nazis found one way after another to strip Jews of their property for years to come. The path that Hitler laid out was clear. A few of the people attending the Steglitz conference had already begun to help individual Jewish

Christians in small ways with money or provisions.

Dietrich saw a much bigger issue. The Confessing Church must not only be concerned for non-Aryan Christians but also step out and help the Jews who were being discriminated against because they were Jews. He wanted the Confessing Church to address the underlying social injustice, not simply help Christian Jews. He called the Jews "brothers of Christians" and "children of the covenant." Most German Christians denied or covered up any links between Judaism and Christianity. Some had even proposed that the Old Testament should be taken out of the Bible to eradicate any connection between Jews and Christians. But Dietrich Bonhoeffer took the Word of God seriously. Rather than deny the link between Jews and Christians, he saw it as a persuasive reason for Christians to become involved in the welfare of the Jews. He had little patience for anyone in the new Confessing Church who might begin to waver in the face of the Nuremberg laws and be tempted to placate Hitler on the Jewish issue. At the conference in Steglitz, Bonhoeffer spoke passionately and in a straightforward manner that gave the Confessing Church no option but to venture into even more dangerous territory.

Every month that went by took Dietrich Bonhoeffer deeper into profound conflict with his own religious tradition. He was already at odds with the established German Church that his country had known for four centuries. Now he risked putting himself at odds with those in the Confessing Church. His willingness to speak directly into the opposition testified to the strength of his passion to follow Christ even in the ethical choices that he faced each day. Bonhoeffer understood accurately the dark days that lay ahead for the Confessing Church.

December 2, 1935, less than three months after

Steglitz, fell on a Monday. Traditionally German newspapers did not publish a Monday morning edition, and few people at Finkenwalde listened to the radio regularly. That evening, a student returned from nearby Stettin with an evening edition of the newspaper. It contained the "Fifth Decree," which declared that an official in the Nazi party would now decide spiritual questions such as ordination and church appointments. Any power that any church administration held was stripped away. No church group of any kind had any power to decide anything about its own affairs; in fact, the Fifth Decree meant that the seminary at Finkenwalde was officially illegal. Yet Dietrich knew that he would stay and keep the seminary open and running as long as possible. He called his students together to explain the Fifth Decree and said each person must make his own decision whether to stay or to go. Everyone, without exception, agreed to continue as usual the next morning. There would be no interruption in their routine until they were forced to stop.[5]

8

A Window of Freedom

In the mid–1930s the Confessing Church, while still brand-new, was in its heyday. Curiosity attracted some to learn more about it. To become associated with the Confessing Church could mean personal risk. Nevertheless, Christians unhappy with the established German church rallied. Contributions to furnish the seminary came from everywhere. Knowing that well-to-do families lived in the region around the school, Dietrich Bonhoeffer lobbied for ongoing financial support as well as food and immediate furnishings. One of the most prominent supporters of Finkenwalde was Ruth von Kleist-Retzow.

Ruth was a widow and a grandmother whose estate was close to the seminary. Three of her grown children were dismayed by how heavily the Nationalist Socialist Party influenced the schools their children attended. The families arranged for all the cousins to live with their grandmother in Stettin, which was fairly removed from the cities of Germany. Some of the schools in the region had so far escaped Nazi influence, and Ruth von Kleist-Retzow's grandchildren began attending these schools while living with her. Ruth supervised school activities, took the children to concerts, spoke French to them at meals, and involved them fully in her political and religious interests. This included the new Confessing Church.[1]

When Finkenwalde opened, Ruth was eager to become involved and met Dietrich Bonhoeffer early on. She had read some of his earlier writings and was impressed with his thinking. So when Ruth had the opportunity to hear him preach on a regular basis at Finkenwalde, she jumped at the chance. She took her grandchildren to services where they heard the robust singing of seminary students and listened to Bonhoeffer's sermons. Several of the grandchildren were in the right age bracket to attend the confirmation classes that Dietrich taught. These connections led to a long and lasting friendship between Dietrich Bonhoeffer and Ruth von Kleist-Retzow. Ruth frequently invited Dietrich to be a guest in her home for tennis or a meal or a theological discussion. Students were free to drop in as they wished. Before long, Ruth was meditating each morning under Dietrich's supervision on the same biblical texts he assigned to his students.[2] One grandchild in particular, Maria von Wedemeyer, was an adolescent at the time, but would grow into a young woman with a prominent place in Dietrich's affections.

In November 1935 the second half-year course of study at Finkenwalde began. This was a particularly dark time for the infant Confessing Church. The very issues that led to their separation from the German Christians—relationships with Jews, for instance— now threatened to divide members of the new church. Every move that Hitler made to strip the Jews of their rights and plummet the country into injustice was a challenge for the Confessing Church to step forward and stand up against the wrong. As personal risk increased under Nazi regime, such bold steps were harder and harder for people to take. Warning signs abounded that the Confessing Church would soon be the target of direct attack by the government. In a sense they were racing against the clock to prepare a group of men to pastor Confessing Church congregations and to make their voice heard in the world beyond Germany.

In addition to running the seminary, Dietrich Bonhoeffer was also giving weekly lectures in Berlin. During this time he struggled with depression, not because he doubted the work he was doing but because the demanding pace was taking its toll on him. Nevertheless, he pushed ahead. In March 1936 Bonhoeffer took his seminary students on a trip to Sweden. This was a bold move. While in Sweden he spoke openly about the concerns of the Confessing Church and the ecumenical movement, even drawing attention from the Swedish press. The publicity caused the Nazi leaders to watch him more closely and look for ways to curtail Bonhoeffer's activities. His popularity and influence began to concern them. When Dietrich returned from Sweden to Germany, he discovered he had unknowingly violated an order issued by the Minister of Education concerning proper authorization for university lecturers to travel outside of Germany. The result was that Bonhoeffer was no longer allowed to lecture at the university in Berlin.

As the Nazi regime crept into more positions of control over the Christian church, Bonhoeffer became more and more involved in trying to stop what he saw. A group of church leaders was involved in drafting a memorandum, which they intended to present to Hitler himself. Although Bonhoeffer was not one of the people who signed the memorandum, he followed its progress carefully. Church leaders consulted him on several points. The memorandum identified specific areas where Hitler's policies caused conflict with the church. The writers were concerned that Hitler was "de-Christianizing" Germany with government policies that were in direct conflict with Christian teaching. These included regulations that virtually required Aryan Germans to act with hatred toward Jews as well as the widespread spying and eavesdropping that the Nazis engaged in. It was clear to church leaders that Hitler intended to silence their voice, and they felt they must protest.

One copy of the memorandum was given to Hitler personally. Officially only two other copies existed. Now the signers waited for Hitler to respond. Weeks passed. Hitler did not even acknowledge that he had received the memo, so the hoped-for response did not come. Suddenly, after six weeks, a London paper published the full text of the memorandum. Someone outside the circle of leaders who had signed the memo had created another copy and supplied it to the London newspaper. The signers had intended only to present Hitler with a simple plea for more reasonable policies. The publication of the memo brought it to international attention and made it seem as if the signers were part of a propaganda plot. All their good intentions were undermined. Now they were on the defensive, knowing that the international embarrassment could lead to drastic action. Dietrich Bonhoeffer discovered that it was one of his own students who had made the illicit copy and sent it to London.[3]

Hitler still did not respond to the memorandum or react to the stir that its publication caused. He had other international issues on his mind that summer—for one, the Olympics, which were only about two weeks away.

The world's eyes were on Germany in late 1935 and early 1936 as the country geared up for the games. The

1916 Olympic Games had been assigned to Germany, but they were never held because of World War I. And because Germany had been such an aggressive force in that war, the nation was not allowed to enter the games again until 1928. Berlin was chosen as the site of the 1936 games before Hitler came to power and began enacting his extreme policies. At the time, Germany was still a struggling democracy. Hosting the games would be symbolic of restoring the country to good favor in the eyes of the world. With Hitler's rise to power, however, many countries questioned the decision. By 1935, after two years of Nazi leadership, the United States and other nations pressed to have the games moved to another place or threatened not to participate. Athletes and politicians around the globe were divided along the line of whether politics should have anything to do with the tradition of sporting competition.

Hitler himself initially opposed hosting the games. Perhaps he viewed them as an interruption to his aggressive agenda. He was interested in restoring German national pride, not in delicate international relationships. But Hitler decided to find a way to use the games to his advantage politically. He came to see the Olympics as an opportunity to present himself as a leader seeking peace and an opportunity to prove the superiority of the Aryan race. He ordered that public displays of anti-Semitism be toned down. There would be no beatings or riots. Hitler wanted the world to see Germany as a peaceful, happy, flourishing country. Although Jews had been excluded from athletic training, now the German Olympic team recruited a German Jew who had left the country to come back and represent the nation in the summer games.

Hitler put on an extravagant display before and during the Olympics. One of his key objectives was to show the world that Berlin—and all of Germany—was an extremely Christian country. He jumped on the bandwagon of seeing Communism, his political enemy, as the spirit of the antichrist the Bible speaks of and wanted the world to believe that Germany was standing up against it. Indeed, Germany was leading the fight against the antichrist himself when they denounced Communism in favor of the National Socialist Workers' Party. The official church set up a huge tent near the Olympic stadium and organized a series of religious services. In addition, they produced a series of scholarly theological lectures at nearby Holy Trinity Church to present Germany as a leader in Christian theological thinking.[4]

The Confessing Church also saw the rare opportunity that came with the Olympiad. Thousands of people would visit Germany for the games. Millions more would follow the games from around the world. The opportunity to influence the thinking and impressions of people everywhere pressed upon the Confessing Church leaders.

As part of his public relations campaign, Hitler temporarily relaxed regulations, and private groups were able to operate more freely. The Confessing Church took advantage of this. Leaders, including Bonhoeffer, were certain that something drastic would happen as soon as the temporary freedom of the Olympiad was over. Dietrich's personal letters written during this time refer to the gathering storm that was sure to let loose as soon as the Olympics were over and the thousands of visitors had gone home. This was an opportunity that would not come again, and they must make the most of it. The Olympiad was their chance, perhaps their last chance, to speak to the world and to be heard unhampered and uncensored. Still they had to be careful, knowing full well the repercussions that

could come later. Some lobbied for a widespread literature campaign to put their message into the hands of
everyone who passed through Berlin—but this also
would put individuals at great risk later. In the end
leadership opted for a moderate approach. They organized a series of talks by leaders at a church with a central location in Berlin. Every day a new speaker took
the podium. While the theological lectures sponsored
by Hitler's government were poorly attended, the Confessing Church lectures were packed at every meeting.
They had to arrange space for the overflow crowds.
With the eyes of the world watching, the Nazis dared
not cause a public display by trying to shut down the
series of lectures.

Dietrich Bonhoeffer was one of the most popular
speakers. Dietrich's topic was "The Inner Life of the
German Evangelical Church Since the Reformation."
On the surface it seemed like a harmless topic. He
wanted to give evidence of the traditional Protestant
forms of prayer. He used a collection of hymns to make
his point, talking about how the words to the hymns
sung in churches reflected the true heart of German
believers rather than the rhetoric of the established
German Church influenced by Nazi politics. Although
he could not know it at the time, this was the last occasion in which Dietrich Bonhoeffer would stand before a
large crowd to speak openly.[5]

Hitler became a profoundly involved Olympic spec-
tator, standing at the rail and watching every competition. At the games, Hitler personally and publicly
congratulated winners of each event, putting on a con-
genial, peace-seeking face to the world. This went well
until the men's high-jump competition. Hitler left the
stadium, for Americans had won all three medals, and
two of the three winners were African-American athletes. And then Jesse Owens, another African-Ameri-

can athlete, won four gold medals. He broke the world record in the 100-meter dash and was just a hair shy of the record in the 200-meter dash. But perhaps his greatest victory came in the long jump. Before the final jump, Owens was tied with a German athlete at exactly 25 feet, ten and a half inches. On his final jump, Owens ended up at 26 feet, five and three-eighths inches, winning the gold. The German, Luz Long, now a silver medalist, embraced Owens, and they strolled around the stadium arm-in-arm. Owens went on to win a fourth gold medal in the 400-meter relay. When prompted to congratulate this outstanding athlete, Hitler was enraged by the very suggestion. Under no circumstances would he allow anyone to take his picture shaking hands with a non-Aryan athlete. Hitler had planned to use the Olympics to show the supremacy of the Aryan race. In the face of the victories of Jesse Owens and other African-American athletes, Hitler retorted that their extreme physical prowess only served to prove that non-Aryans were closer to animals than men.[6]

For those two weeks of August 1936, Adolf Hitler's dictatorship camouflaged its extreme militaristic campaign. Nazi leaders used the games to bedazzle foreign spectators and journalists. They presented a picture of a peaceful, tolerant Germany. Internally, the public relations campaign fueled German national pride and contributed to Hitler's continued popularity. Preparing for the international event had brought industry and jobs. Visitors to the country, to a large degree, saw what Hitler wanted them to see. Had the countries embroiled in the question of mixing politics and sports opted to boycott the Berlin Olympics and bring further attention to the atrocities in Germany, perhaps history would have taken a different path. Some believe that doing so would have caused Hitler to reevaluate what he was doing and would have bolstered international resistance to the Nazis. But no one boycotted the games, and with political politeness behind him, Hitler plunged again into policies leading to world war.

As Berlin emptied of its international visitors, and the glamour of the Olympiad faded, reality returned to the tension between the Nazi state and the Confessing Church. The unacknowledged but published memorandum to Hitler was still a hot issue. In the churches debate raged about whether the entire document ought to be read from the pulpits of Confessing Church congregations. In August a modified version was issued, and suddenly a million copies were in print. Hitler had achieved many victories in 1936 in military campaigns and foreign and economic policies. Yet the church leaders dared to criticize him openly. They took some precautions, however. Church leaders decided to send Dietrich Bonhoeffer to a conference in Switzerland that he had not planned to attend, but to which he agreed to go. The timing of the conference coincided with the designated Sunday that the memorandum would be read from pulpits. If the Nazis decided to take drastic action against the Confessing Church because of the memorandum, church leaders would have a representative outside of Germany with wide international contacts.[7] Still Hitler did not respond. And the Confessing Church waited, knowing that sooner or later Hitler would find a way to make things still more difficult for them.

9

The Tightening Net

The post-Olympic crackdown that the Confessing Church anticipated came right on schedule. With international attention turned elsewhere, Hitler resumed his aggressive policies toward any groups who opposed him. The Confessing Church was a prime target. The principal method to put a muzzle on these Christians was to develop an intricate network of regulations for all churches. The Ministry of Church Affairs directed these regulations under Hitler's authorization. Churches were forbidden to hold gatherings of any sort on nonchurch property or emergency locations. This law targeted Confessing Church congregations in particular. Many of these were located in towns where a government-approved German Christian congregation also existed. The German Christian congregations held the official church buildings and did not suffer greatly under this ruling. In contrast, Confessing churches often did not have traditional church buildings to meet in, and the new law made their makeshift meeting places illegal. The Ministry of Church Affairs also made duplicated communication subject to Editorial Law, which meant the Ministry could censor or disapprove any church communication with multiple copies. This included the newsletter that Dietrich prepared for his students and other small publications of the Confessing Church. The net around them clearly was tightening.[1]

The Olympic year was the first and only full year of operation for the seminary at Finkenwalde. The next year teaching there was considered illegal. In July 1937 a wave of persecution affected people related to Finkenwalde. Former students wrote personal letters to Dietrich that told of having their houses searched, being held for lengthy periods of questioning, and having their personal belongings confiscated without notice or reason. More than two dozen former students were arrested. Dietrich wrote detailed letters to all their relatives. He also arranged for some of their young wives to stay with his good friend Ruth von Kleist-Retzow on her estate near Finkenwalde.[2]

The final term came to a close in September 1937. Bonhoeffer was away from the seminary on holiday when he received a telephone call saying that the Gestapo had arrived. Because the term had finished, no students were at the seminary. The Gestapo found only the housekeeper and the director of studies. Both had to leave immediately, and the Gestapo sealed the doors.

Dietrich's first impulse was to rush to Berlin and protest. When he arrived, the streets were filled with celebration of Hitler's alliance with the Italian leader Mussolini. For several weeks he intensely fought the order to close the seminary. But by mid-November it seemed clear that the order was final and irrevocable. Lawyers and petitions used up all his time and energy, but nothing changed. Finkenwalde would not reopen. In fact, other small seminaries around the country were forced to close as well. Bonhoeffer now turned his attention to his students. In the circumstances that many of them faced, they might be tempted to give up the disciplines he had taught them. It would be too easy to stop resisting the government's takeover of the church. While they lived in community they could support each other. Now they were scattered around the country. Many of them wrote to Dietrich. He answered their letters promptly and personally in his own handwriting. He also began a circular letter that all his former students could read. This was the beginning of a carefully guarded newsletter to Finkenwalde students.

A total of 150 students had graduated from half-year courses under Dietrich Bonhoeffer's tutelage. Some wanted to continue to study with him despite the closure of the seminary. The Confessing Church was entering a period of trial with an uncertain end, and Dietrich wanted to do what he could to continue training young pastors.

The answer to this dilemma, at least for a while, was a sort of apprenticeship. Some ministers who held legal positions in the German Christian Church secretly supported the Confessing Church. Bonhoeffer's students could be placed as apprentices in these churches with a fair degree of safety. The Nazis had not yet challenged apprenticeships in these situations. Leaders of the Confessing Church sought out pastors who already served churches sympathetic to their cause. Each Finkenwalde student was registered with a pastor in good standing with the government and was officially on the staff of the church. In reality, students were in a period of in-pastorate training. Whenever possible, students were placed in churches clustered together so that they could conveniently gather in a central location for group instruction. Students lived together even more frugally than they had at Finkenwalde. They set up temporary group housing in vacant parsonages around the region. Dietrich traveled around to teach these "collective pastorates" for as long as possible. His own life became increasingly unsettled. He could not teach at the university to support himself, and Nazi officials had banned him from living in Berlin, where his family was located. He had no permanent residence during this period of time, because he was never in the same place for more than three days a week. But with so many students and former students to stay in touch with, contact became more and more difficult. Dietrich wrote letters in his own handwriting and marked them "personal" in order to keep them legal, but many letters were meant for groups of people to read.

The heyday of Finkenwalde had come to an end. Though it had a brief existence, the seminary had a profound influence on Dietrich Bonhoeffer personally and, through him, on the wider Christian church. The two and a half years that he spent living in a regulated Christian community played a vital role in Bonhoeffer's development as a Christian and as a theologian. He wrestled personally with the issues that he impressed on his students: practicing personal spiritual disciplines; what it means to live in relationship to others; making ethical choices that please God; matching theology with real-life events and decisions. The experience of living in community significantly influenced Bonhoeffer's writings as well. Had Finkenwalde never existed, Bonhoeffer might never have written some of his most prominent works, such as *The Cost of Discipleship* and *Life Together*. The closure of the seminary in 1937 led to the publication of both of these volumes sooner than Bonhoeffer had first intended. Regardless of how it had come to an end, the experiment of communal life was over; he had written all he could about it. Now it was time to publish. *The Cost of*

Discipleship was in print before the end of the year.

Another important outcome of the Finkenwalde experience was Dietrich Bonhoeffer's relationship with Eberhard Bethge, one of his students. Eberhard became Dietrich's assistant. They were close personal friends at Finkenwalde, and their relationship endured the terrors of the years yet to come. After Bonhoeffer's death, it was Eberhard Bethge who pieced together the manuscript Bonhoeffer had worked on in prison called *Ethics*. Eberhard also preserved the letters that Bonhoeffer wrote to him prolifically over the years, especially while in prison. Eberhard Bethge married one of Dietrich's nieces, extending a deep friendship into a family connection. Much of what is known about Dietrich Bonhoeffer's life and thought came through the work of Eberhard Bethge and the relationship that began at Finkenwalde.

Also during the Finkenwalde years Dietrich Bonhoeffer began to consider personal involvement in organized resistance to Adolf Hitler. February 1938 brought an opportunity for Dietrich to add action to his words. His brother-in-law Hans von Dohnanyi approached him with an offer that required yet another bold step. Hans and Dietrich had been friends for years and were very close. Hans had never had anything to do with the Nazi Party. He was a well-known lawyer employed in the German justice system before Hitler's rise to power. In May 1933, after Hitler had taken control of the country, von Dohnanyi was assigned to the Reich's Ministry of Justice. His position gave him a close-up view of the Nazi regime, and he began to document their outrageous actions. This journal would play a vital role in events that would unfold years later. In February 1938 Hans introduced Dietrich to four leading figures of the German resistance. As Hitler's policies became more severe and extreme, more and more German people found them unacceptable. But because Hitler ruled in a dictatorship, there was little that could be done through normal constitutional or legal channels to oppose Hitler. Hans was not introducing Dietrich to a small fanatical band that went against popular views. In fact, what he organized in secret resistance against Hitler more and more represented the view of the people that the dictator was going too far. By now Hitler had been in power more than five years, and while Germany had flourished economically, and patriotism was on the rise, his treatment of Jews increasingly became an issue that demanded confrontation.

As Dietrich learned more about the activities of this secret group, he wrestled with questions of Christian ethics in the context of Germany. He asked himself, "Who stands fast?" The answer formed in his mind over several years: the final standard is not reason or principle or conscience or freedom or virtue. Many people who have been measured by these standards have fallen short. For Dietrich Bonhoeffer, the question was one of obedience and allegiance to God. The ones who "stand fast" spend their entire lives answering the call of God, in whatever form it takes.[3] Ideas lead to decisions, and choices result in actions. While wrestling with these questions, Dietrich continued traveling, teaching, and leading the Confessing Church.

Hans's involvement in the resistance deepened. He drafted a written challenge for a general in the army who believed that Hitler's plan for aggressive military action was wrong. The general was to present the challenge to the highest-ranking official heading up Hitler's army. The resistance movement hoped that the challenge would make the highest military leaders think again about supporting Hitler's plan. But the general hesitated and did not present the challenge.

On March 11 the Italian leader Mussolini agreed not to try to stop Hitler's plan to take over Austria. The very next day Hitler moved into Austria. The invasion of this neighboring country was more like a parade than a military triumph. The Austrians seemed to welcome Hitler, and he took the country without bloodshed. The world watched, aghast, as Adolf Hitler got exactly what he wanted with virtually no resistance. Without evidence that Hitler planned a widespread war, how could a military official argue against his policies? Hitler's popularity increased. The moment to challenge Hitler had passed.

Dietrich Bonhoeffer watched these events carefully. While he was not personally involved in resistance activities, more and more he began to support them. Dietrich and Hans were now convinced that anyone hoping to stop Hitler would have to be in a position of power. Attempts to stop him through changing laws were pointless; Hitler controlled the laws. Attempts to stop him by stirring up international opinion against him had not worked; the international world had been slow to respond, or in some cases agreeable to what Hitler was doing. A more direct approach, it seemed, was to gain influence in the army, at whatever cost.

This was a drastic change in thinking for Dietrich Bonhoeffer. Until this point, he had argued that people must summon the courage to say no to Nazi policy and be willing to accept the consequences, even if it meant losing their positions. Standing on principle was important to him. Now he was convinced of the urgency of stopping Hitler. It was important to keep people of character in positions of power. If that meant saluting Hitler or camouflaging the real purpose of a person's activities, this was now acceptable to Bonhoeffer. He was no longer offended when Dohnanyi and others kept in close contact with people at the heart of the

Nazi Party. Hitler was deliberately leading Germany into widespread war. The Jewish question was intensifying in a way that Bonhoeffer could not tolerate. It was time for someone to take action. If they were going to remove the lion, they had to be in the lions' den.[4] Bonhoeffer's roots were deeply embedded in pacifism. It was no easy decision to decide to endorse a course of action that was not based on pacifism but that, in fact, might lead to violence.

In April 1938 Hitler ordered clergy serving in church positions to swear an oath of allegiance, faithfulness, and obedience to Adolf Hitler as they carried out the duties of their office. No new pastors could be appointed without swearing allegiance to Hitler. Those called into ministry before the decree went into effect had to take the oath retroactively to remain in their positions. Because Dietrich technically was employed by the Old Prussian Council and was not serving in a pastoral position, he was not required to take the oath. But many others in the Confessing circles had to face the decision. Meetings of pastors during those weeks were tense and full of conflict. Some argued that taking the oath was justified in order to continue serving. Dietrich Bonhoeffer argued that allegiance belonged to God alone, and insincerely swearing an oath of allegiance was a serious step. Many Confessing Church pastors gave into the weight of pressure and took the oath to Dietrich's dismay. He knew that once again Christians would confront the question of Aryans and Jews. Swearing allegiance to Hitler would mean swearing allegiance to a belief that, for Dietrich Bonhoeffer, was clearly against the teaching of Scripture.

Dietrich knew that his brother-in-law Hans was secretly working to overthrow Hitler, and that under the dictatorship and a perpetual state of emergency, no laws held Hitler back. The constitution was abandoned, the legal system suspended. Conspirators saw no hope of influencing Hitler to be more moderate or to bring change through political systems. Hans was convinced that more drastic action was needed: Hitler must be forcibly removed. He thought Bonhoeffer could help do that.

10

Domination and Oppression

I t was 1938, and Hitler had been in power for five years. Germany was a very different country than it had been. The humiliation of defeat in World War I was behind Germany, and Hitler had succeeded in jump-starting both German national pride and the economy. The standard of living—at least, for Aryans— was rising. Germany's military power was becoming a threat, feared by other countries in Europe. Hitler's military machine marched on.

In the summer months the intense persecution against the Jews mounted until it once again touched Dietrich personally. His twin sister's Jewish husband, Gerhard, could no longer earn a living. The threat of violence against Jews increased daily, and Gerhard faced more risk every day that he remained in Germany. Hans von Dohnanyi was emphatic that the situation would soon become even worse, as impossible as that seemed. The Ministry of Justice, where he worked, was in a frenzy of activity rewriting laws so that passports would identify Jewish people. Since the Jews had already been declared second-class citizens,

78

losing a legal passport would close the last door to escaping Hitler's reign of terror. Sabine and Gerhard made the painful decision to leave Germany on September 9, 1938. Both Hans and Dietrich helped make the arrangements. Dietrich still had many contacts in London, and he mobilized them now to find help for his sister. He made sure his friend George Bell would settle the family and use his influence to help Gerhard find work. They loaded up two cars in a way that looked as though they were going on a short family holiday. Sabine and Gerhard drove their family car with their two daughters in the backseat. Dietrich and his good friend Eberhard Bethge, who was closely connected to the family by this time, took another car to accompany them as far as they could. The four adults rotated so that they all spent time with the children. Although the girls were young, they sensed that this wasn't an ordinary family trip. Their mother's morning request that they wear two sets of clothes was strange, and they were missing school. Nevertheless, they liked the attention they were getting and spent a lot of the time singing favorite songs. The refugees stopped for a picnic supper along the way. After the meal, the tone changed. Dietrich and Eberhard now turned back, bidding an uncertain farewell to Sabine and her family. Sabine and Gerhard planned to cross the border into Switzerland before midnight. In a few hours they were safe in Zurich.[1] A few weeks later they traveled on to England. They had left Germany with the hope of returning, but in less than a month their passports were declared invalid. They could not go home. They would have to settle in London, away from their families, without knowing if it would ever be safe to return to Germany.

Hitler pressed ahead with his plans to dominate Europe. After his invasion of Austria six months earlier, the political powers of the world knew what he was doing. Hoping to avoid a full-scale war, world leaders negotiated with Hitler. On September 30 British Prime Minister Chamberlain agreed not to interfere with Hitler's plan to take over a portion of Czechoslovakia. In exchange, Hitler promised that he would not be aggressive toward any other country. He had Austria, and if he could have a portion of Czechoslovakia, he would reach his goal of reuniting the parts of Europe that had once belonged to the great German empire. He marched his armies into Czechoslovakia just as he had Austria six months earlier, without resistance.

Hitler made no promises to the world about his treatment of German Jews, however. In November he brazenly attacked the Jews by orchestrating Kristallnacht, or "Crystal Night." Organized acts of violence against the Jews called "pogroms" had been happening since the early centuries of Christianity. But not since the Middle Ages had a government endorsed and promoted a pogrom. This is what the Nazi regime did under Hitler's orders. On a designated night, private citizens and police took whatever action they wished against Jewish businesses, organizations, and individuals. Synagogues and cemetery chapels throughout Germany burst into flames. Under strict orders, police did not interfere with these "protests." On a single night, riotous looters smashed their way into more than seventy-five hundred Jewish-owned shops. The name Kristallnacht signified the broken glass of shattered shop windows. Although the Jews were the victims and not the attackers, police arrested more than twenty thousand Jews overnight. Hitler ordered police to arrest as many as the existing prisons could accommodate. Then prison officials received orders to contact concentration camps prepared just for this occasion and arrange to transfer the "prisoners." The concentration camps made famous by World War II were now open and taking new residents. Jews, already nervous and frightened, were openly terrorized by permission and endorsement of the German government. Countless unprovoked beatings of Jews happened that night, and nearly a hundred Jews died. Then officials began liquidating Jewish bank accounts and taking over the private property of Jews. Hitler ordered that the Jews themselves pay the cost of the repairs to the damaged buildings. He declared the amount to be an astronomical 250 million dollars.[2]

Dietrich Bonhoeffer was in a remote area of the Pomerania region with some of his students on November 9, still trying to run an illegal underground seminary. He was not immediately aware of the night of terror that signaled a level of persecution against the Jews in Germany from which the country could not turn back. In ignorance of the event, Dietrich moved from the seclusion of one group of students to another. There he discovered that the second location had been the site of one of the "protests." As he grasped the extent of the wreckage, his students sheepishly admitted that they had stayed in the safety of their rooms. They did nothing to protest or stop the burning of the Jewish synagogue in their town. Bonhoeffer expressed his severe disappointment. In his grief over the events, he opened his Bible to Psalm 74 and underlined the words of verses 8 and 9: "They burned every place where God was worshiped in the land. We are given no miraculous signs; no prophets are left, and none of us knows how long this will be." Next to this passage, Dietrich wrote the date of the horror: November 9, 1938. This was the only time he ever put a date in his Bible to mark an event. The date also marked a turning point for Dietrich personally.

Bonhoeffer's mind now turned with more interest to

the activities of his brother-in-law Hans von Dohnanyi and the determination of a growing number of people to stop Hitler before he destroyed the country they loved and plunged all of Germany into the immoral beliefs that fueled his commands. In the months since Hans had introduced him to resistance leaders, Dietrich had thought heavily about the implications of joining the group. No one had yet gone so far as to plan to assassinate Adolf Hitler. Rather, leaders of the conspiracy against Hitler hoped to force him out of leadership through legal means. They wanted to arrest him and hold him publicly accountable for what he had done. One possible strategy to remove him from office was to have him certified as mentally ill. Hans suggested that Karl Bonhoeffer, Dietrich's father and still a leading psychiatrist in Germany, could write the report. The conspirators could take this report to army generals who sympathized with them and were in a position to act on it.[3] Conspirators had to be absolutely certain that they had key people in key positions before attempting to put this plan into action.

Hans moved into a new job that put him in an even better position to help with such a conspiracy. In 1939 he began working for the Abwehr, the secret military intelligence agency of Germany. He acted as a private secretary to Admiral Canaris, who was the head of the Abwehr and who had been working steadily for years to move Hitler out of power. Early in Hitler's regime, Canaris had hoped he could help steer Hitler away from the evil he saw developing. By 1938, however, he had given up on this and was devoted to helping conspirators in the German army carry out a coup that would force Hitler out of power. Canaris was prepared to use the Abwehr to help this cause. He had a great deal of power and made a firm decision about how to use it.

Because the Abwehr was the heartbeat of German military intelligence, it was the one organization in all of Germany that was largely out of reach of the Gestapo police. As the Nazi party expanded, Gestapo officials were not happy with this arrangement. They watched Canaris closely, and he watched them closely. But he covered his tracks well. As hard as they tried, the Gestapo could not find anything to hold against Canaris. They had no information to use as a reason to take over the Abwehr. When Hans von Dohnanyi began working for Canaris, he had access to information about both Nazi strategies and changing laws and the activities of the groups trying to remove Hitler. Hans shared information freely with Dietrich Bonhoeffer.

At that point in time, Dietrich was not directly involved in any of the conspiracy activities. But Hans and others did turn to Dietrich for counsel about ethics and understanding biblical passages. Dietrich was becoming the "conscience" of others who were considering drastic action against Hitler. Many of the people in the conspiracy against Hitler were committed Christians, as was Dietrich, so it was not easy to entertain using violence to accomplish their objectives. Dietrich himself had been a determined pacifist who did not believe that violence, even between nations, ever settled anything. In the wake of Hitler's unjust dictatorship, Dietrich began to move toward believing that action was, in fact, urgently needed. The people in the position to take action would have to wrestle with the implications of their choices. Hans once asked Dietrich what he thought about Matthew 26:52, where Jesus said, "All who draw the sword will die by the sword." Dietrich's response was that the verse was still relevant. It was true even for the circle of people who were trying to remove Hitler. He believed that the time had come for certain individuals to take responsibility for deciding the verse's meaning for themselves.[4] Whether he meant to be or not, Dietrich Bonhoeffer found himself caught up in the web of strategy and conspiracy to remove Adolf Hitler from power by whatever means necessary.

11

Escaping the Draft

G ermany mobilized for war. The Germans knew
it, and the world knew it, despite Hitler's
promise not to invade other countries once he
had Czechoslovakia. Whether war was officially
declared or not, Hitler was building up his army, and it
was only a matter of time before men born in 1906
would be called into service. This would make Dietrich
Bonhoeffer eligible for military service against his will.
His work of visiting and encouraging his students
became next to impossible to carry out, and it would
not protect him from being drafted. But he had virtually no other options for employment within church
structures, since the Nazis had taken over all church-
related decisions. Dietrich urgently needed to find
some means of supporting himself that would also keep
him out of military service.

Hans von Dohnanyi was using his connections to
try to find something for Dietrich. Time was running
out. Although overseas travel required government
permission and risked calling attention to himself, Dietrich decided to pursue this option. He contacted
Bishop George Bell in England, who had helped him

get his sister Sabine's family out of Germany. In March 1939 he went to England. His official purpose was to visit relatives, which was a legitimate reason to travel. While he was there, he met with Reinhold Niebuhr, an American theologian he had met as a student in New York in 1930. Niebuhr began making arrangements for Bonhoeffer to be invited to New York for speaking and teaching.

Dietrich made most of the arrangements to go to America by correspondence. Because Nazis censored mail in and out of Germany, letter writers could not always communicate plainly. An American group had arranged for Dietrich to work for the Federal Council of Churches. His responsibility would be to work among the German refugees in New York. He would also have opportunity to teach at Union Theological Seminary, where he had studied earlier. He could accept other preaching and speaking invitations as he wished. What Dietrich did not understand before arriving in New York was that the Federal Council of Churches expected him to stay perhaps as long as three years. Despite the enormous difficulty of living and working in Germany in 1939, Dietrich Bonhoeffer did not intend to stay away so long. He was concerned that he might not be allowed to return to Germany. For weeks he struggled with internal conflict. While he did not judge others who decided to leave Germany, he was not at peace with that decision for himself. A complex network of people had gone to a lot of trouble to make arrangements for him to come to America and to have something meaningful for him to do. Disappointing them was the furthest thing from his mind, but Dietrich was miserable in America. And within a few weeks he knew that he could not stay. His choice was one of integrity. How could he do the right thing if he was in the wrong place? Staying in New York without a full commitment to the work there would be hypocritical and deceitful. Despite the dangers, returning to Germany would be the truthful, obedient thing to do.

Dietrich wrote to his sister Sabine of his dejection. He had hoped that teaching in America would be a refreshing experience—no police breathing down his neck, freedom of movement and speech, no hostile government to confront. Instead, Dietrich found it was too difficult to be away from Germany, and he certainly could not make a commitment to stay in America for three years. Even if Hans had not yet found a plan that would keep him out of military service, Dietrich wanted to go back. He believed that he would have no right to take part in rebuilding the church in Germany after the war if he did not continue to share in its trials during the war. So within six weeks of arriving in America, he left. He stopped in England for a few days to visit his twin sister. They could not know it then, but they were never to see each other again. Dietrich was back in Germany by the end of July.

Two months later Hitler broke his promise to the world and attacked Poland. Britain and France now declared war on Germany. World War II had begun. Hitler moved swiftly to expand the army, forcing young men of military age into uniforms. His determination to succeed was quickly rewarded. Poland surrendered on September 27, 1939. Hitler ordered the army to prepare to invade Holland and Belgium as well. The conspirators against Hitler wanted very much to believe that army generals would now stand up against Hitler rather than help lead Germany into another world war. But what if they didn't? More and more, Dietrich Bonhoeffer needed a way to stay out of the army.

Hitler planned to invade countries west of Germany on November 12, 1939. Although the world may not have known the exact date, Hitler's military preparations were obvious. The Abwehr, on the other hand, made it their business to know the details of Hitler's plan. The conspirators still hoped to prevent this act of war and made preparations of their own.

One of the generals involved suggested that Hans von Dohnanyi update his records of Hitler's evil actions and include as much detail as possible. This information would be crucial to a later step in the conspiracy strategy, and it must be complete and up to date. The conspirators' plan was to arrest Hitler and let the people of Germany see a side of Hitler that they did not want to admit existed. Most people saw only the public figure of a national leader who charmed them with his promises of prosperity and pride. The conspirators believed that if people knew the true facts about Hitler, they would change their minds. The chronicle of evil that Hans assembled could enlighten millions of people to this truth.

At the same time, generals who wanted to overthrow Hitler also wanted to protect Germany. They were concerned that other countries would hold all of Germany responsible for the crimes of the Nazis. Through their international contacts, they sought a promise that countries such as England would treat Germany differently once Hitler was out of the way. Dietrich Bonhoeffer had been working on the same issue through his ecumenical contacts in other countries. The resisters did not want to overthrow Hitler so that they could have power of their own. They wanted the best for Germany, and they believed this included peaceful relationships with the nations of the world. Unfortunately, world leaders would make no such promises. Hitler's hold on power showed no sign of weakening. Against that reality, world leaders were not interested in discussing compromise and cooperation with a group that had not proven they were able to remove Hitler.

As the date for attacking Holland and Belgium approached, the generals got nervous. In the name of patriotism, they were about to do something that others would call treason. If the plan was not carried out successfully, their own lives would be destroyed. They planned every detail until they were virtually positive they could not fail. But the risk was tremendous. The one general who was to give the command for the coup to go into action got cold feet. It seemed that Hitler might have heard rumors of the plans. If this was true, and Hitler was able to identify who was involved, he would come after them with merciless vengeance. The chance was too great that Hitler already knew too much information for the plan to succeed. If the plan were launched but failed, everyone connected to it would be executed. The general destroyed any written evidence that the plan existed or that he was involved.[1]

The conspirators began working on another plan.

12

Invasion of Western Europe

As winter weather set in, Hitler delayed his invasion of countries to the west and finally postponed it indefinitely.

In early 1940 the conspirators, now including Dietrich Bonhoeffer, tried another approach. Hans continued making a detailed record of the atrocities of Hitler and the Gestapo. He also worked on a new document that urged the army generals to act quickly. Bonhoeffer joined the exclusive group that met at Hans's house to work together. They labored over every word of the document, every step in the plan. Their efforts, however, did not get the reception they had hoped for.

With the coming of spring, Hitler once again pressed ahead with his strategy to invade countries to the west. His generals were busy with their responsibilities for the invasion and hesitant to have anyone think they weren't fully behind the plan. Even though some generals disapproved of Hitler's intentions, they were not willing to appear the least bit hesitant to follow orders. Hitler kept his generals too busy to have time to look at the conspirators' plan without bringing suspicion upon themselves.

The commander in chief of the army received the document but set it aside. The clock ticked on. Each hour that passed shrunk the possibility that their action would thwart the invasion of the Netherlands and Belgium. In Bonhoeffer's opinion, the people who were capable of acting suffered from "paralysis of the conscience."[1]

On May 10, 1940, German armies invaded the Netherlands, Luxembourg, Belgium, and France.

As war and rumors of war raged around him, Dietrich Bonhoeffer continued to respond to God's call. Hitler had eagerly responded to France's declaration of war, and with more success than world powers had expected. Nazi armies pressed across France and sent back reports of victory. Even in this context, Dietrich lived out his commitment to the Confessing Church. His technical employment with the Abwehr actually gave him the freedom to continue his work of training pastors. Though the net tightened around the Confessing Church, Dietrich pressed ahead boldly, unwilling to quit until it became physically impossible to continue.

In the afternoon of June 17, 1940, Dietrich had just come from a pastors' meeting. The evening would bring a Confessing Church service at which Dietrich would preach. In between, he spent the afternoon hours with his student and friend Eberhard Bethge in an open-air café in the village of Memel, Germany. The summer sun was warm on their faces as they ate. Suddenly a fanfare erupted from the café loudspeaker. In a few seconds came the announcement that France had surrendered to Germany. People all around leaped to their feet, some even jumping onto the tables in their patriotic enthusiasm. Dietrich rose as well, but with different thoughts racing through his mind than most of the people around him. Arms up and down the street went up in the Hitler salute that Dietrich had detested and resisted for so long. But today Dietrich's arm went up as well.

Eberhard Bethge stared at him, unbelieving, as Dietrich urged him to raise his arm.[2]

Bonhoeffer was ready to live a double life—outwardly. In the past he had looked on with grave disappointment as others in the Confessing Church considered making concessions to the Nazis so that the church could continue its ministry. He had argued that the Confessing Church must put its stake in the ground and be willing to stand apart from the culture that accepted Nazi leadership. He knew that such actions involved risk. The consequences could be severe. But he believed it was the right thing to do. Compromise was an unacceptable choice.

Time and experience had molded Bonhoeffer's thinking. The end goal became more important than the action of the moment. He continued to oppose Adolf Hitler and everything that the Nazi Party stood for. But it was becoming increasingly clear that standing on principle over a salute might mean Hitler would continue to rise. Instead, Dietrich now believed, Confessing Church leaders and others who opposed Hitler would continue to take risks, but for far more significant issues. He was now willing to give the outward appearance of fitting in with the people around him who were enthusiastic about the pride and victory Hitler was bringing to Germany. A salute meant nothing. And this outward appearance might mean the difference between being able to oppose Hitler in more meaningful ways and being stopped completely, thus clearing the road for Hitler to press ahead even more aggressively. Bonhoeffer's inward integrity remained intact even as outwardly he moved from a position of pacifism toward active involvement in the resistance against Hitler.

June 17 marked the success of Hitler against France, but it also marked the failure of hope for a peaceful removal of Hitler from power. Many who opposed the dictator, whether in the church or in the military, believed that once Hitler had to fight real battles he would face defeat. He had taken Austria and part of Czechoslovakia without opposition or bloodshed. Surely Hitler would meet a stronger power, and his regime would come to an end. But the victory in France only a month after Hitler's attack brought an end to that hope. Hitler's hold was more solid than ever and showed no cracks. People like Dietrich Bonhoeffer had to rethink their position. If Hitler was not going to be removed in the short term, how would they live honorably under his rule in the long term?

On September 4, 1940, Dietrich Bonhoeffer received word that the Reich Central Security Office had issued an order that prohibited him from making any public speeches. This included sermons. Anything that came out of Bonhoeffer's mouth was considered subversive activity. He was also ordered to report to the police regularly. They wanted to know where he was and what he was doing at all times. Any teaching activity was out of the question under these circumstances.

Hans went into action. He had been working on a plan to save Dietrich for months, and now everything was in place. He had arranged for Dietrich to work with the Abwehr. And now he was to be a civilian agent in the network of military intelligence. As an employee, he would be sent on assignments that were officially Nazi business. But his real work was for the conspiracy to overthrow Hitler. Admiral Canaris and others in the Abwehr were very interested in the international contacts that Dietrich Bonhoeffer had in ecumenical circles. He was virtually the only person in Germany who could build bridges between the conspiracy against Hitler and the international efforts to oppose the German leader. The Abwehr set him up with an official address in Munich, but he lived in a Benedictine monastery, where he was largely left to himself and could come and go without interference. Dietrich also had protection from Gestapo investigations, because the Gestapo was not allowed to interfere with the Abwehr or to know any of its military secrets. Dietrich Bonhoeffer, a pacifist at heart, who thought of himself primarily as a pastor, was now an active player in the resistance against Hitler. He expected success. He expected to be around to help rebuild the German church after the war. But he also knew that this work carried great risk. Hitler would have no mercy on anyone caught opposing him. None of that mattered. Dietrich was ready to put feet to his faith, to pay the cost of discipleship no matter how high.

Under the protection of the Abwehr, Bonhoeffer could also travel quite freely. More than once someone who did not know of his work for the Abwehr wondered how a humble pastor got permission to come and go as often as Dietrich did. But he put every trip to good use. Through his widespread international contacts, Bonhoeffer tried to convince the nations opposing Hitler that Germany would be different without the dictator, and their attitude toward Germany as a nation must be different than their attitude toward Hitler. No matter what Hitler might say, he did not represent the heart of the German people. Dietrich's strategy was to convince leaders in ecumenical circles of this. They, in turn, could put pressure on their national leaders to come to the aid of Germany rather than hold the country responsible for what the dictator did. Members of the conspiracy against Hitler hoped that international pressure against Hitler could save Germany from the evil direction it was heading. Despite several years of such work, Dietrich did not have much success. More and more he was convinced that direct action against Hitler would be necessary and justified.

It was not difficult to have Dietrich declared "indispensable" to military intelligence. The argument was that military intelligence worked with all people, even Communists and Jews. Why should they not also work with the Confessing Church? The Abwehr was able to suspend the orders for Dietrich to report to the police at regular intervals. In reality, Bonhoeffer was now freed up to concentrate on his theological work in the quiet setting of the monastery outside Munich.

In this context, Dietrich Bonhoeffer began spending regular time on what he saw as the major theological work of his life: *Ethics*. For weeks at a time he worked in a peaceful setting. Never before had he enjoyed such a lengthy period for studying, reflecting, and writing. Bonhoeffer considered the study and presentation of ethics as the main task of his life. Certainly he had been called to give counsel on ethical decisions in the issues that the Confessing Church faced. Individuals involved in the conspiracy against Hitler went to Bonhoeffer as they sorted through the rights and wrongs of what they contemplated. Certainly he made his own decisions about what was right and wrong in the progressive phases of his own opposition to the Nazi regime.

Writing *Ethics* was an enormous undertaking. Unfortunately, Bonhoeffer never got to complete the manuscript. Large portions of it survived in fragments after his death, but Bonhoeffer himself never got to edit and arrange them. Nevertheless, we see in these pages the utter prominence that he gave to the lordship of Christ in ethical decisions. Bonhoeffer was not interested in writing theology merely for academic purposes. His concern was always that theology should pervade and undergird experience. Theology must be relevant to the events going on around Christians. This is the context for making Christ-centered ethical choices.

13

Awakening Love in the Midst of Turmoil

In 1941, the Abwehr put Dietrich Bonhoeffer to work. The journey from pacifism to resistance was complete. Bonhoeffer was not hiding under false protection of the organization; he was willing to carry out assignments that would help bring down Adolf Hitler. In February he went to Switzerland for a month to renew relationships with ecumenical church leaders. High-ranking officials in the German army still hesitated to take action against Hitler. In the wake of his aggression against the nations of Europe, they wanted assurance that world leaders would not retaliate against Germany once Hitler was removed. As Nazi troops stormed around Europe, however, this was less and less likely. Nevertheless, Dietrich went to several countries to meet with church leaders who might be able to influence their own governments. If the Allied nations would give some sign of support to the conspiracy against Hitler, then the German generals might be bold enough to take action. Dietrich's travels continued into 1942 and included Italy and countries in Scandinavia as well as Switzerland.

Shortly after returning to Germany from Switzerland in 1941, Dietrich had received a letter that said he had neglected to apply for membership to the writers' guild before publishing his books. If he had any hope of publishing again, he had to join the guild and pay a disciplinary fine for publishing without joining. Soon he received another letter that said his application to join the writers' guild was denied. Because he had been prohibited from speaking in public because of subversive activities, now he would not be allowed to publish either.[1] Clearly the Nazi regime wanted to make Dietrich Bonhoeffer as useless to the Confessing Church as possible. He could not teach at the university. He could not stay in Berlin. He could not speak in public. He could not publish his work.

At this point Bonhoeffer became more and more involved in the plot against Hitler. With the protection of the Abwehr, he could still travel quite freely. In fact, some of those he visited wondered how he could get permission to travel as much as he did. Of course, they did not know of his involvement with military intelligence. Rumors circulated of large-scale "euthanasia" of the Jews. Stopping Hitler became imperative, even if world powers would not guarantee kindly treatment toward a Germany without Hitler. The German blitz against England from July to October 1941 made that powerful nation uninterested in cooperating with groups to overthrow Hitler. England and other world powers now wanted Germany to surrender completely, with no terms of compromise.

In September 1941 Hitler ordered people of Jewish descent to wear an identifying yellow star on their outer clothing. A few weeks later the rumors of "euthanasia" came true as the first trains full of Jewish individuals rumbled toward the East. Whole Jewish families were taken from their homes in the middle of the night and deported. Undercover work to help Jewish people and to remove Hitler rose to critical proportions. Success could mean the difference between life and death on a daily basis.

Hans von Dohnanyi began organizing a plan to get a small number of Jews out of Germany safely, and he recruited Dietrich to help. They supplied legal papers to Jewish individuals that identified them as foreign agents officially working for military intelligence. The plan was called "Operation Seven," though eventually they helped fourteen people leave Germany and arrive safely in Switzerland. Eleven of the people were Jews who had become Christians. The other three had not converted. It made no difference to Dietrich Bonhoeffer. Some in the Confessing Church were more inclined to help Jews who had become Christians. Dietrich believed that all Jews were being treated unjustly, and Christian disciples were compelled to do something to help. Hans, Dietrich, and others involved planned carefully, meticulously looking at every detail. It was critical that all the papers were above reproach. Any indication of their real purpose must be thoroughly hidden. A special challenge came with the task of providing money to the fourteen Jews who had left Germany. Bank transactions leave trails. Financial ledgers must match up. Withdrawals of official funds required explanations. Hans was exact and thorough in everything he did. Still he could not know how this act of charity would impact his own destiny two years later.

In June 1942 Dietrich Bonhoeffer had just returned from Sweden, where he had met with his old friend Bishop George Bell from England. Dietrich went to visit Ruth von Kleist-Retzow and enjoy a period of rest. While he was at the country estate familiar from his Finkenwalde days, Dietrich met Ruth's granddaughter. Dietrich barely remembered meeting Maria von Wedemeyer years earlier. She was an adolescent living with her grandmother during the Finkenwalde days, not even old enough for confirmation. Now she was a young woman who caught Dietrich's eye. She had just graduated from high school and was visiting her grandmother, with whom she had always had a close relationship. She had been there only a few days when Dietrich Bonhoeffer came to stay. At first she was a bit put off by the theologian whom her grandmother held in such high esteem, but soon the three of them were getting along quite well. Dietrich could not help but notice that Maria had become a lovely young woman, and he began to develop an affection for her.

Late in August word came that Maria's father had been killed in a battle at Stalingrad. Bonhoeffer went once again to Stettin, this time to offer sympathy to the family. Ruth had undergone an operation on her eye, and Maria was taking care of her. Bonhoeffer visited often in the weeks after that. Maria turned to him for help coping with the loss of her father and the danger that swirled all around them. Dietrich found Maria charming and graceful and full of the traits he had come to admire in other members of her family. She was smart-minded, inquisitive, and attractive.

This unexpected courtship continued in the weeks that followed as Bonhoeffer came and went from Ruth's estate. War and grief swirling around them, Maria and Dietrich fell in love and began planning a future together. By November he was ready to speak to Maria's mother and to seek an official engagement. While Maria's mother liked Dietrich, she was not sure that her eighteen-year-old daughter could truly understand what it would mean to marry a man whose political and international involvements were complex. Dietrich had repeatedly stood up against both the Nazis and church leaders. Could Maria really know what she was getting into? Frau von Wedemeyer proposed that they wait one year. During this year they should not see each other. At the end of the year, if they still wanted to marry, she would give her blessing.

Dietrich did not hesitate to say no to this proposal. He was certain of his feelings. Maria was certain of hers. They wanted to be engaged. Despite her reservations, Maria's mother gave in, and on January 17, 1943, Dietrich and Maria became engaged. For now, though, they agreed to keep the engagement quiet and postpone any public celebration. They did not set a definite date for a wedding, but they were glad to have settled between themselves that they would one day marry.

The happiness that characterized Dietrich's personal life at this time contrasted sharply to what was happening in the conspiracy circles. The Gestapo was not happy to leave the Abwehr beyond its reaches. There is no evidence that the Gestapo suspected that Canaris and his military intelligence organization were involved in a conspiracy against Hitler, because Canaris had covered his tracks well on that issue. But the Gestapo began to search for any small piece of information, any minute indiscretion, any transgression at all that would give them opportunity to rattle the Abwehr and take over.

14

Failed Coup Attempt

Shortly after Maria and Dietrich settled the question of their engagement, the other side of Dietrich's life intensified. The plot to remove Hitler became more complex. A peaceful coup was impossible. The army generals clearly were not willing to risk their own lives and reputations without assurance that Allied nations would give them a chance to rebuild Germany peacefully. As Hitler's forces pressed on, the Allied nations clearly were not going to make any promises. The inner circle of conspirators, which included Dietrich's brother-in-law Hans von Dohnanyi, began making plans of another kind. If Hitler could not be removed with an army coup, he must be killed. They wrestled with their consciences. Hans consulted Dietrich, who had come to believe that assassinating Hitler was a justified ethical choice. At Christmas 1942 Dietrich wrote an essay entitled "After Ten Years," which he sent to family and friends. This short piece put into words the question he had been asking himself for years: "Who stands fast?" Dietrich examined the question of resistance to the government and how far the conspirators might be justified in going. In Dietrich

Bonhoeffer's mind, resistance was ultimately grounded
in his allegiance to God above anything else. Hitler was
a pervasive evil that disguised and obscured true moral
values. The men involved in the inner conspiracy circle
had nothing to gain personally from overthrowing Hitler. They were above reproach in their motivations.
Each of them had a sense of both relationships and
responsibilities, and perhaps Dietrich Bonhoeffer more
than any others. He had a strong conviction of living in
relationship with other people. His choice to be
involved in the conspiracy against Hitler did not arise
from personal interests; he had nothing to gain. He
was not going to become the next leader of Germany.
He was not an army general waiting in the wings for
recognition and power. His actions were the outcome of
his ideas and convictions. As human beings we live in
relationship to other human beings. God created us
this way. In the incarnation, when God became human,
God showed us grace in our world. As we live in relationship with others, we must show God's incarnate
grace in our actions. This means living in responsibility to others as well as in relationship with them. Dietrich Bonhoeffer believed this meant being willing to
sacrifice his personal welfare in order to show God's
grace in the world. The people involved in the conspiracy believed this. Their rebellion against Hitler was a
rebellion of their Christian consciences. Dietrich Bonhoeffer rejected any discussion of moral values that put
God "above" and humans "below." His theology was
rooted in the incarnation of Christ. God had come into
the world. Christians are God's people in the world, living in obedient discipleship.[1]

On March 13, 1943, when Hitler entered his plane,
a small parcel of fused time bombs was on board. As his
flight progressed through the air, the conspirators
waited anxiously to hear of success. Instead, they met

with the news that Hitler's plane had landed safely in East Prussia. The ignition on the bomb had failed to start.

Conspirators immediately turned their attention to another opportunity only a few days later. Hitler was scheduled to inspect an arsenal as part of the observance of Heroes' Remembrance Day. A major in the army was prepared to carry two bombs in his coat pocket and make sure that they blew up at just the right moment, even at the cost of his own life. The whole procedure was carefully timed. Hitler was scheduled to spend thirty minutes on the inspection. This would give the major time to get in the right position close to Hitler at a certain point in time. Once there, he would ignite the fuse that would set off the bomb and take Hitler's life.

It was a Sunday afternoon. The Bonhoeffer family was gathered with all the grandchildren in the home of Dietrich's sister Ursula. In a few days Dietrich's father, Karl Bonhoeffer, would be seventy-five years old. The family planned a large celebration. On that day in Ursula's house, the grandchildren were practicing a cantata that they would sing for their grandfather on his March 31 birthday. Dietrich himself was at the piano, playing beautifully while others sang or joined with other instruments. This was something the Bonhoeffer family did often. For nearly everyone there, this was an ordinary Sunday afternoon family gathering: music, food, enjoying the grandchildren. But in one corner Hans von Dohnanyi kept looking at his watch. Once the fuse was lit and the bomb exploded, he would receive a phone call to confirm that it was all over. Outside, Hans had his car ready to leave. The conspirators would then launch into a phase of renegotiating international relationships and rebuilding the German nation into a country they could once again be proud of.

But the call did not come. Later Hans discovered the heartbreaking explanation. Hitler had unexpectedly changed the schedule, finishing his inspection in only ten minutes rather than thirty. The major had not had time to get in position to light the bomb.[2] The window of opportunity was closed.

The conspirators looked for another window. By now they knew they were racing against time. The Gestapo was looking for a way to shut down the Abwehr. If they succeeded, they would also shut down the core of the conspiracy. Bonhoeffer had been planning further trips abroad, but he had been cautioned not to travel just then. Drawing attention to himself in any way could jeopardize the network of resistance. No one involved in the plot against Hitler must give the Gestapo any reason to look at anyone more closely.

A routine customs search in Prague turned up an "irregularity" in a financial transaction. The trail quickly led to individuals who had knowledge of Operation Seven from the year before. When interrogated, they gave answers that incriminated more people, including Hans and Dietrich. The Gestapo turned its investigation to the activities of the main offices of military intelligence. Admiral Canaris entered a standoff with the Nazi security officers. Canaris insisted that the affairs of military intelligence must remain secret. Nazi officers suspected that something was amiss but could not yet prove it. The financial "irregularity" they had stumbled upon accidentally was just what they needed to fuel their determination to break down the Abwehr.

Hans and Dietrich began feverishly to weave a web that would protect them as long as possible. Hans went to Switzerland to make sure that the trail of docu-

ments and financial matters related to Operation
Seven was impeccable. Then he and Dietrich worked
on a document that would prove that Dietrich Bonhoeffer was indispensable to military intelligence opera-
tions. If they did not succeed in this, Dietrich would
certainly be required to enter the German army. Dietrich wrote a long letter to Hans offering to share his
international information with the Abwehr. Hans
made sure that Dietrich had the exact kind of paper
that was used two years earlier. Dietrich put the letter
on that paper and dated it November 4, 1940, in
Munich. The letter made it look as if Dietrich had two
years earlier offered to hand over all his ecumenical
contacts to Hitler's leadership of the war.[3]

The Bonhoeffers went ahead with the family celebration of Karl Bonhoeffer's seventy-fifth birthday.
This would be the last family occasion for Dietrich.

On April 5, 1943, Dietrich telephoned his sister
Christel, Hans's wife, from his parents' home. A
strange male voice answered the phone. Without
speaking, Dietrich quietly replaced the phone in its
cradle. He knew at that moment that the Gestapo had
arrested Hans and Christel. It was only a matter of
time before they would come for Dietrich as well.

Chief Investigator Manfred Roeder informed Admiral Canaris that he intended to have Hans's office
searched. Not all of Hans's notes made it to safety.
With the Gestapo present, Hans and his co-workers
had no opportunity to speak directly to each other.
They used a sort of code that they had agreed to use if
this kind of circumstance ever arose. However, not
everyone understood the messages the same way, and
the Gestapo observed an officer seeming to hide a slip
of paper. The paper contained proof that the Abwehr
had been involved in treasonous activities. Still Hans
tried to make it seem as if it had a different signifi-

cance and that the information on it was all part of a military intelligence code. Admiral Canaris supported Hans in declaring the paper official business, and for the moment the incriminating evidence was set aside. But the Gestapo did not lay their suspicions to rest. They arrested Hans and later picked up his wife, Christel, at their home.

When Dietrich realized what was happening, he went upstairs to his attic room in his parents' home and tucked the *Ethics* manuscript under the beams, where he hoped the Gestapo would not find it. He destroyed other papers that might incriminate him or others involved in the conspiracy to overthrow Hitler. Then he carefully placed some false documents on his desk, where the Gestapo would be sure to find them. Calmly he went next door to his sister Ursula's home and asked her to prepare him a large meal. After he finished eating, he returned to his parents' house. At four in the afternoon, two men in a black Mercedes arrived to arrest him and take him to Tegel Prison in Berlin. He did not resist.

Police took Christel and Hans separately to two other prisons. Hans, Christel, and Dietrich were interrogated separately under conditions whereby they could not possibly try to coordinate their stories. However, they had known all along that arrest was a very real risk, and they had planned their strategy ahead of time. Although the Gestapo had discovered the trail of Operation Seven, the Abwehr had covered its tracks so well that it was difficult to pin the crimes involved on any one person. The Gestapo recognized that Hans von Dohnanyi was at the center of Operation Seven. Their interest in Dietrich Bonhoeffer was simply that he was a close associate of Hans. Under pressure, he might crack and give them information they needed to prosecute Hans.

With the arrests of Dietrich and Hans, and others involved with Operation Seven, the entire circle of conspirators fully understood the breach that had come with the failures of the attempts on Hitler's life. The Gestapo's early interest was in Operation Seven and their belief that it was a cover-up for helping Jews and not a truly military intelligence operation. Gestapo leaders did not understand that by arresting people involved with Operation Seven they had smashed open the conspiracy's center of activity. No matter how much the conspirators had prepared ahead of time, there was always the risk that under interrogation and torture, someone answering questions about Operation Seven would say something that would lead the Gestapo to the true purpose of Canaris's operation—the removal or assassination of Adolf Hitler. So far Canaris was still in command of the Abwehr, but clearly its protected status was at risk.

Karl Bonhoeffer successfully used his connections to arrange for the release of his daughter Christel fairly quickly. After all, she was not technically an employee of the Abwehr and had not been charged with anything. Her only "crime" was that she was married to Hans, who was the key target of the arrests. Christel was released, but Hans and Dietrich remained at separate prisons.

Tegel was a military interrogation prison. When he arrived and was taken to his cell, Dietrich could not even bring himself to touch the wool blankets on the wooden bed. Their stench was overwhelming. In the next cell, someone wept loudly. Dietrich could do nothing to reach out and bring comfort. In the morning, guards tossed dry bread through a crack in the door. They had been instructed not to speak to the new arrival. Dietrich sat in his cell not knowing how long it might be before interrogations began or how long he might remain in Tegel. In his mind he rehearsed the strategy he had agreed on with Hans and the others. Hans would take as much of the responsibility personally as possible. He would try to make others, including Dietrich, seem insignificant to Operation Seven. Dietrich would present himself as a humble pastor who had offered to serve his country with his international connections. He had carried out his assignments for the Abwehr just as they were given to him and no more.

The long prison wait had begun.

15

Making the Most of Confinement

At Tegel prison Dietrich Bonhoeffer soon learned to concentrate on what he could do and not consume himself with worry or frustration over what he could not do. He thought of the first few weeks of his imprisonment as tiresome but temporary. When questioned, he stuck to his story that he was an inexperienced pastor who had only tried to help his country. He was confident that at another military prison in central Berlin, Hans was running rings around his interrogators. Chief Investigator Roeder was in charge of the cases against both Hans and Dietrich and shuttled between the prisons. So far Dietrich had not been charged with anything. Roeder questioned Dietrich only to glean information that he could use in a case against Hans. But when Roeder came periodically to interrogate Dietrich, the young pastor could tell that the chief investigator was getting nowhere in his attempt to break Hans's will.

In these early weeks, nothing bothered Dietrich more than not being able to see Maria. He was in Berlin; she was at her grandmother's in the countryside.

Even if she were in Berlin, she would not be allowed to see him. He was not even allowed to write to her with the assurance that he was well. Maria got some photographs of Dietrich from his mother and kept those in front of her whenever she wrote to him or read his letters to his parents.

Dietrich kept himself physically fit by exercising in his cramped cell and eating whatever nourishing food his family was able to send in to him. And he knew how to be friendly with the guards. They found him an interesting prisoner and were soon agreeable to special requests. He took advantage of the privilege of receiving books and read extensively during these months. Dietrich certainly had plenty of time to study and think, and he used it to try his hand at writing in various formats—poems, drama, even a novel. As often as he was allowed, he wrote letters. At first, this was only one letter every ten days. He was also allowed an hour's visit with a family member once a month. However, a guard who took a liking to Bonhoeffer offered to smuggle extra letters in and out. Many of these survived him and contribute to what we know about Dietrich Bonhoeffer's prison years. In addition to their letters, family and friends also sent bundles of clothing and food, which the guards passed on to Dietrich.

At the end of June, with very little prior notice, Maria finally got permission to visit Dietrich. And he had only a moment's notice that he would see her. Guards brought Dietrich to a security office, where they could clearly hear everything the couple said. He thought Maria was incredibly brave to have come. He would never have suggested to her to do something so difficult. She wrote later that Dietrich was visibly shaken at the sight of her. It was obvious to both of them that she was being used as a tool to break Dietrich's will. At first he said nothing. Then he began what he hoped sounded like a normal conversation. His words showed no emotion, but what he felt came through the pressure that he put on Maria's hand as he held it.[1]

Maria visited again at the end of July. Dietrich was decidedly more calm and relaxed this time. They talked about trivialities. What more could they say to each other with Gestapo guards listening to every word? They talked of the weather and driving and family news. But she looked into his eyes and saw the light in them and knew that Dietrich was all right.[2]

Despite the difficult circumstances, the relationship of the engaged couple flourished. They had so little time together and had to be so careful what they said. The touch of a hand or a light in the eye said more than a thousand words. Dietrich wrote to Maria as often as he was allowed, filling his letters with hope for their future, words of tenderness and personal reflections on the meaning of the trials they endured. They wrote of their wedding, thinking quite optimistically that they would not have to wait much longer. Dietrich would be released, they would be married, and they would have a long life together.

Dietrich's hope for a future with Maria was partially fueled by news from the outside about the progress of the war. On July 10, 1943, Allied forces landed in Sicily, and fifteen days later the Italian leader Mussolini was overthrown. Hitler could no longer depend on support from that relationship. Though he had tried to build military alliances of his own, more and more he found himself battling Allied forces on the strength of just the German army. Armed forces of nations committed to victory over Germany pressed closer every day. While Dietrich had worked toward a victory over Hitler that would not penalize the entire nation, an end to the war by any method would be welcome and would surely lead to his release. So the couple remained hopeful for Dietrich's freedom and a future together.

From April to July, Dietrich faced periodic interrogations. Though he had been in prison nearly six months by that time, it was not until September 5 that he was "officially" put under arrest and charged with a crime. It was up to Dietrich to find himself a lawyer. He could write a letter every four days now, instead of every ten, and he was permitted to write directly to Maria, though he was sure these letters were being read before she received them. Often his letters took more than ten days to reach her, even after she had moved to Berlin to be closer to him and to facilitate more frequent visits. Dietrich alternated writing letters to his parents and then to Maria. And his parents shared many of their letters from him with Maria. Letters arrived erratically, sometimes several bundled together. Clearly the censor officers were reading them first. But the correspondence eventually became steady and bolstered them both.

Toward the end of September, Dietrich's lawyers managed to persuade Manfred Roeder not to charge Dietrich with high treason as Roeder intended. They even managed to get Roeder transferred to other responsibilities so he could not press forward with his personal suspicions. Dietrich was, however, charged with undermining the morale of the armed forces, and this was a serious enough charge to deal with. Dietrich perhaps recognized the gravity of his situation when he made out a will on September 20, 1943.[3]

The trial date was set for the middle of December. Dietrich was hopeful that he would be home for Christmas. The prosecution had no solid evidence that Dietrich Bonhoeffer was directly involved in any suspect activities. He was impeccably consistent in presenting himself as understanding very little of the activities of the military intelligence agency for which he worked. He did not try to invent a web of lies that Roeder could untangle and use to hang him. The Gestapo had no proof of a conspiracy. They had no proof that Operation Seven was anything but a routine military intelligence operation. They had no proof that Dietrich knew anything more than what he had told them upon his arrest. Dietrich stuck to a bare bones story that allowed him to be truthful about his involvement without incriminating Hans or anyone else.

When he began receiving books, Dietrich also received covert messages from his family, messages that would not be read and censored by the guards or Roeder himself. As part of preparing for the possibility of imprisonment, Dietrich's family had worked out a code system. Beginning in the back of a book, every second page would have a letter with a scarcely visible pencil mark under it. Dietrich was to read from the back of the book and decode the message. If he wished, he could send a book back to his family with another message.

Over time Dietrich Bonhoeffer enjoyed a level of freedom in the Tegel prison that most of Hitler's victims did not enjoy. Although Tegel was a military prison, not everyone working there supported the Nazi regime. It didn't take Dietrich long to discover the guards who objected to Hitler's policies and were sympathetic toward efforts to change them. Other guards were willing to be "helpful" if prisoners or their relatives showed "kindness" with a stream of gifts. It is because of the humanity of a few guards that we know as much as we do about Bonhoeffer's time in Tegel and what he was thinking about during that time. He received notepaper from the guardroom for his writing.

Guards carried extra correspondence in and out of Tegel at their own risk. They also gave him privacy when he had visitors, such as Maria or his friend Eberhard Bethge. When Eberhard married Dietrich's niece, a guard carried out a written wedding sermon to be read during the ceremony.[4] All through the months at Tegel, Dietrich held to a daily routine of reading the Bible, praying, and meditation. He was glad that he knew so many hymns by heart.

When December came, Hans was too ill to stand trial. He suffered from severe rheumatism and could barely walk. The trial was postponed. The months that followed were full of hope that a trial would come soon, and Dietrich remained optimistic that the prosecution could not prove anything against him. Nevertheless, clearly he was going to be in prison over Christmas. He wrote a Christmas letter to Maria in which he reaffirmed his fervent belief that his life was in God's hands, not in human hands. Even what seems evil and dark can be good and light because it comes from God. We do not always see as God wants us to see.[5]

In February a new round of interrogations began. Dietrich interpreted this to mean that at last a new trial date would be set. But now it seemed that Hans's strategy was to delay trial until Allied forces could arrive to remove any risk of a guilty verdict. Hans asked his wife, Dietrich's sister, to send him food infected with diphtheria. She did so, and he was once again too ill for trial. As the March date for trial came and went, Dietrich settled into accepting Hans's strategy. Evidence against them was not strong. Allied forces were pressing closer all the time. The case would simply run out of steam and they would be released.

In the meantime, Admiral Canaris was relieved of his command and placed under house arrest. The Gestapo had stumbled onto enough information to sus-

pect an organized conspiracy, though they could not yet
prove that Canaris was part of it. Canaris continued to
explain away any suspicious piece of information. For
example, as head of military intelligence, Canaris
would naturally have his hands on all sorts of information, including information that was unflattering to
Hitler. Finding such documents within his organization meant only that he was doing his job. The Gestapo
could prove nothing.

Maria came to visit at the end of March 1944. She
gave Dietrich a detailed account of the Bonhoeffer family celebration of his father's seventy-sixth birthday,
marking a year's time since the failed attempt on Hitler's life and the beginning of the Gestapo investigation
into the Abwehr.

Against unbelievable odds, Hans and Dietrich managed to have indirect communication. The conspiracy
circle, though shaken up by the arrests of Hans, Dietrich, and others, had not abandoned their efforts.
Another attempt on Hitler's life was planned for July
20, 1944. Whether Allied victory came first or the
death of Hitler came first, Dietrich believed that the
end of his imprisonment was in sight.

During these prison months Bonhoeffer renewed
his theological work. He worked further on his *Ethics*
manuscript and sent sections of it out to family for
safekeeping. His imprisonment prompted him to
explore even more fully than ever before the significance of the presence of Christ. He focused on the lordship of Christ, who exercised his powerlessness
through service, even the cross. For Bonhoeffer, the
suffering and powerlessness of Christ was the center of
everything. His major concern was always how Jesus is
present with us.[6] In a situation where he might have
felt abandoned by God, Dietrich Bonhoeffer felt the
nearness of Jesus even more.

16

Hitler Survives Another Attack

We can only imagine how much the prisoner of Tegel cell 92 looked forward to July 20, 1944. Conspirators planned another attempt on Hitler's life. Dietrich Bonhoeffer knew that the date would be a watershed moment for Germany. Although he had no direct involvement in the plans for that date, the outcome would determine Dietrich's future. Success would mean the certain release for the scholarly prisoner and, even more important to Bonhoeffer, he would at last be free to help rebuild the Christian church in Germany with the Bible as the foundation rather than Nazi policy. Army leaders could try to negotiate peace with the rest of the world. On the other hand, word of failure would bring an unspeakable outcome. Bonhoeffer placed himself in God's hands.

The plot to assassinate Adolf Hitler, long in the planning, was outlined to the smallest detail. The method. The time. The delivery person. The risks. Several previous attempts to stop Hitler's climb, even at the cost of his life, had been unsuccessful. Each time the stakes got higher. The Gestapo had already stumbled onto the core of the conspiracy, even if they did not realize it. The slightest slip-up could lead the Gestapo to the conspirators and shut them down permanently. The cost to Germany would be enormous.

In June 1944, Colonel Count Claus Schenk von Stauffenberg became the chief of staff to General Fromm, commander of the reserve army. Stauffenberg was a war hero with a sterling reputation and unquestioned loyalty. With this new assignment, he was frequently present in meetings with Hitler. No one would suspect him. He saw that he was in a unique position to take action where other high-ranking army officials had gotten cold feet. Stauffenberg began to calculate his opportunities. Soon he volunteered to personally carry a bomb into a routine conference with Hitler.

On July 20, 1944, Stauffenberg carried an ordinary-looking briefcase into a conference room in East Prussia. Twice on the way in someone offered to carry his briefcase for him. Stauffenberg politely refused the offer. As they entered the room, however, Stauffenberg finally had to surrender the briefcase. Hitler shook his hand when he entered the room, which was full of Nazi officers—two dozen people altogether. Everyone expected Stauffenberg to give a report when called upon. Stauffenberg acted as he normally would; he asked to be seated as close to Hitler as possible in order to hear well.

The unsuspecting officer who had the briefcase now set it down to Hitler's right, but a good distance from Hitler. It was an ordinary briefcase. No one would notice it. Stauffenberg knew that the briefcase was not as close to the Führer as he would have liked, but the clock was ticking. The timer was set for ten minutes, and though the location of the briefcase was critical, Stauffenberg had no opportunity to move it. Knowing that time was running short, Stauffenberg excused himself from the room, left the building, and crossed the compound.

What Stauffenberg did not know was that another officer found the briefcase in the way of his own work and moved it. Still no one suspected anything unusual. But now the briefcase was under a massive oak table at which Hitler and others were working. Suddenly an explosion tore through the air in the middle of the day. A bluish-yellow flame spiraled upward above the conference room. Glass and wood fragments flew through the air. Voices cried out for doctors. By this time, Stauffenberg was getting into a car to return to the airfield and fly back to Berlin. When he saw a body carried out on a stretcher covered by Hitler's own cloak, he assumed Hitler was dead.[1]

The bomb had gone off as planned. Three people were killed, one of them carried out under Hitler's cloak. But Adolf Hitler himself survived. The massive oak table that Stauffenberg had not counted on saved Hitler's life. The blast temporarily damaged Hitler's hearing, but he had no lasting injuries. The treasonous attempt launched Hitler's rage anew. Hitler went on the radio at one o'clock in the morning and vowed vicious revenge. He immediately ordered widespread investigation. Stauffenberg's trail was not difficult to trace. Believing that his effort was successful, he had not been particularly careful about covering his tracks on the way back to Berlin. The very next day the Gestapo organized eleven fact-finding teams. With more than four hundred officers dedicated to finding people linked to a conspiracy against Hitler, the bloody rampage began. An enormous wave of arrests occurred. Stauffenberg, who believed he had acted out of patriotism for his country, was shot as a traitor. Soon the net widened to capture dozens of others connected to the conspiracy against Hitler, some already in prisons and others at large.

No one was safe. As soon as word filtered to Tegel prison that the July 20 coup attempt had failed, Dietrich Bonhoeffer knew the end was at hand for him. It would only be a matter of time before the investigation would make a firm connection between his name and the circle of conspirators. Whether or not he had anything to do with the July 20 attempt did not matter. He had associated with a group of people intent on overthrowing, and later killing, Adolf Hitler. The angry Nazi regime would not spare his life on a technicality, and Dietrich knew that. Still he put himself in God's arms. He wrote to his good friend Eberhard Bethge that "we must cast ourselves into the arms of God" and take seriously the suffering of God in this world. Dietrich's concern was not for his own suffering, even at the moment when his death seemed inevitable. Rather, he felt in his heart the suffering of Christ in this world. To Bonhoeffer, that was true faith.[2]

Dietrich marked off the days until October, knowing that on any one of those days his life could end. By now Allied forces were bombing Germany, even Berlin. It was still possible that the war could end before Hitler finished systematically destroying all those who had plotted against him. As Nazi and Allied forces raced against each other, Dietrich Bonhoeffer could do nothing but wait and rest in the arms of God. The "cost of discipleship" was never more real to him than in those slow-moving weeks. The Holy Spirit's inner transformation of Dietrich Bonhoeffer brought deeper faith and maturity in the difficult days, without regret that he had stood up to the evil of Hitler. Gradually he sent most of his possessions out of his cell, including books and manuscripts he had been working on. He kept only his most current theological project before him, sending everything else to safety.

Dietrich's family did not stand by idle. They went into action making every contact they could. Their hope was to make a plan for both Dietrich and Hans to escape. They smuggled the plans into the Tegel prison and found a sympathetic guard. One of them was willing to cooperate with an escape plan. All the details were ready for early October. Dietrich would leave the prison wearing a boiler suit. As the violence closed in around him, and all hope of a fair trial gone, Dietrich agreed to the escape plan. His parents supplied the suit. The guard was ready. At the last minute, though, Dietrich learned that his brother Klaus had been arrested, along with their brother-in-law Rudiger Schleicher. Klaus and Rudiger had become involved in the plan for a coup only after Dietrich and Hans were imprisoned. But their arrests put the escape plan in a whole new light. Dietrich could not think only about what would benefit him. What would happen to Klaus if Dietrich escaped under the noses of the Gestapo? Dietrich feared that his escape would bring increased suffering to his brother still in prison. He called off the escape plan. In only a matter of days he faced the personal consequences of that decision.

Dietrich's days at Tegel came to an end, as he knew they would. Gestapo officers arrived and escorted him to an underground cell at the Central Security Headquarters in Berlin. Bonhoeffer's prison experience fundamentally changed at this point, becoming much more typical of Gestapo imprisonment. Breakfast and supper were a mug of weak coffee and two slices of bread and jam. The midday meal was usually soup. Food portions were small. Prisoners appreciated the shower at the end of the hall. Although the water was cold, going to the showers gave them a chance to whisper to each other. Dietrich's parents and Maria had more difficulty getting food packages delivered to him, but they persisted in their efforts to do everything they could. At Tegel Dietrich had fallen into a comfortable, predictable rhythm of communication both with his parents and with Maria. They were able to get permission to visit him every few weeks. Now that system was almost completely shut down. Some of their packages got through, but they were not allowed to see Dietrich face-to-face. To combat the strain and the long difficult days of interrogation, Dietrich kept himself disciplined with a strict schedule of theological work.

The Gestapo began a fresh round of interrogations. They were no longer concerned with proving that anything about Operation Seven was improper. They had evidence that connected Dietrich Bonhoeffer to a plot to assassinate Adolf Hitler. The "Zossen Files," the detailed chronicle that Hans von Dohnanyi had kept, had fallen into Gestapo hands. On close reading, the files revealed enough about the plans for a coup to lead the Gestapo to both von Dohnanyi and Bonhoeffer. Now the Gestapo knew the true reason for Dietrich's trips abroad on behalf of the Abwehr in 1942. They knew now that even at the high level of Admiral Canaris members of the Abwehr were using their positions to work against the Nazi regime and not simply for legitimate military intelligence. Dietrich had traveled to make international contacts to help the conspirators overthrow Hitler, not to help the success of Hitler. With the Zossen Files, the Gestapo had the proof they needed.

We know little about Dietrich's time in this underground prison. One of Maria's cousins was also a prisoner there at the same time. He later described Dietrich as cheerful, friendly, and optimistic. Dietrich was the one who gave encouragement and hope to other prisoners, reflecting the personal hope that he held in Jesus Christ, no matter what his outward circumstances were.

After a period of time in a concentration camp, Hans von Dohnanyi was brought to the same prison where Dietrich was. He and Dietrich had not seen each other or spoken directly since their arrest on April 5, 1943, more than a year and a half earlier. Hans was now paralyzed in both legs. Dietrich searched for an opportunity to see his old friend even under these impossible circumstances. When Allied bombers were overhead, guards took the prisoners who could walk to a concrete air-raid shelter. Hans was always left in his cell, immobile. Once, on the way back after the alert was over, Dietrich managed to slip away from the group, dart into Hans's cell for a hushed conversation and rejoin the group. No one ever knew he had been gone. But in those precious few minutes Dietrich and Hans agreed on all the important points to make in their statements when they were interrogated. Then Hans returned to the concentration camp, and he and Dietrich never spoke again.

17

A Dark Day in April

Dietrich Bonhoeffer now faced a charge of high treason and conspiracy to assassinate a government leader. No lawyer in the country would be able to get the charge changed. Dietrich knew that. And Hans's strategy of stalling a trial date for the Allied forces to free Germany from Hitler's grip had come to a disastrous end. While everything else in Germany was rapidly disintegrating into complete chaos, the Gestapo went into high gear, taking action against anyone associated with the conspiracy.

On January 12, 1945, Russian troops attacked Hitler from the east. The violence threatened the area where Maria's mother lived, and Maria left Berlin to help her mother close up her home and go to a safer place. When Maria returned to Berlin on February 12, she learned that Dietrich was gone.

A few days before Maria's return, on February 7, Dietrich received a parcel and a letter from his parents. They were present at the prison, hoping to see him. The guards took the parcel and delivered it to Dietrich but turned away the elderly Bonhoeffers. This letter, meant to be his birthday letter for that year, was the last he ever received from his parents. At midday on the same day, Dietrich and nineteen other prisoners were given a few minutes to collect their personal belongings and get ready to leave that prison. The group included many distinguished individuals, among them foreign leaders from Belgium and Austria as well as former German leaders. Admiral Canaris, who had been removed from the Abwehr and arrested, was also in the group. Guards took the prisoners to Buchenwald, a concentration camp. Their quarters were an underground bunker beneath houses originally built for camp officials. It was cold, damp, and dark. The prisoners saw no daylight.

In the same month, Klaus Bonhoeffer and Rudiger Schleicher were sentenced to death. Dietrich's hope of sparing their suffering by increasing his own had crumbled.

When Maria returned to Berlin and discovered Dietrich was gone, she followed him to Buchenwald. She got as far as an appointment with the man in charge of the investigation, but she was turned away without seeing Dietrich, and she never saw him again.

Allied forces pounded the German army. The race against the clock continued. Seven weeks passed in the bunker. On April 1, Easter Sunday, Dietrich and the other prisoners heard the sounds of Allied guns, and their own hopes rallied briefly. But the Gestapo responded to the imminent enemy threat by stepping up their efforts. They had found Admiral Canaris's own diaries and had all the information they needed to convict him of treason. By this point, it was clear to the world that Allied forces would defeat Hitler's armies any day. The Nazi regime was over. It was only a matter of time before the country would find itself at the mercy of international powers. Still Hitler refused to surrender, determined to create as much vengeful chaos as possible before the end.

Two days after Easter, Dietrich's name was called. Once again he had only a few minutes to gather what few belongings he still had with him. With a dozen or so other prisoners, Dietrich boarded a huge, closed-in truck. He spent the next seven days rumbling through southern Germany, not knowing for sure where the truck was going. On April 5, two days into this voyage and two years into Bonhoeffer's imprisonment, Hitler received word that Admiral Canaris's diary had completely exposed the Abwehr's involvement in the plot against the dictator. Hitler's right-hand officer, Himmler, gave orders for the immediate execution of anyone associated with the July 20 plot against his life. The list clearly included Hans von Dohnanyi and Dietrich Bonhoeffer. Their days of stalling against the inevitable were over. As Allied forces closed in, Hitler again stepped up his revenge.

The truck carrying a load of prisoners rolled through the countryside. As evening approached, the weather and roads worsened. Suddenly the truck skidded and lurched to a stop. A quick inspection revealed that the steering mechanism was broken. It would be impossible to have it repaired in the dark and rain. As morning dawned on April 6, the guards let prisoners out of the truck to stretch for a few minutes. The guards had sent for a replacement bus, and when it appeared, they loaded the prisoners on it to continue the journey. A new group of guards took over the duty of transporting the prisoners. They wound their way to a rural school building. Inside, the rooms were warm and dry—with real beds. Dietrich had not slept in a real bed for two years! Food was still scarce, but the atmosphere turned lively for a few hours.

Sunday arrived again, April 8, the Sunday after Easter. Some of the other prisoners pressed Dietrich to hold a brief service for them, which he did. He read the Scripture texts assigned for the day and meditated on them aloud for the small audience. Isaiah 53:5: "By his wounds we are healed." And 1 Peter 1:3: "In his great mercy he has given us new birth into a living hope through the resurrection of Jesus Christ from the dead." Dietrich read and spoke words of hope. And he believed what he read and spoke despite the immediate circumstances.

Only a few minutes after the service, a guard called, "Prisoner Bonhoeffer, get ready and come with us!" All the prisoners knew what that meant. Dietrich did as he was told. He made what he knew were his final preparations to leave this world. He still had a few books with him, and he chose one that he wanted his old friend Bishop George Bell in England to have. He gave the book to a fellow prisoner who was from England, hoping that the new friend would survive to give the book to the old friend. Inside the book he wrote, "This is the end—for me, the beginning of life." Dietrich Bonhoeffer was confident of the world he would soon enter.

Guards took him to yet another camp, Flossenburg. Officials hastily set up a court. Without a proper trial or legal representation, Dietrich Bonhoeffer was declared guilty of high treason before the day was over.

In the gray dawn of Monday, April 9, Dietrich Bonhoeffer prepared for his own execution. A camp doctor, who did not know who Bonhoeffer was at the time, found Dietrich on his knees in prayer. As he looked on, the doctor was moved at the peacefulness he saw in Dietrich Bonhoeffer, even in the moments preceding certain death. As he climbed to the gallows, Dietrich paused to pray once more. The doctor later described him as calm and composed and said that in all his years as a doctor, he had never seen someone die so completely submissive to the will of God.[1] Dietrich was hung on the gallows that gray morning. His body was immediately cremated and his ashes scattered.

Dietrich Bonhoeffer had lived his life exploring the "this-worldliness" of Christianity. He never accepted the notion that Christian faith was separate from living in the real world, even at the moment of his death. His personal faith had guided his sense of civic duty, leading him to take action against an immoral regime. On April 9, 1945, Dietrich Bonhoeffer paid the cost of such discipleship with his life.

Within days, Allied forces liberated the Flossenburg camp. On April 30, knowing that he had been defeated and would be captured at any moment, Adolf Hitler took his own life. The war was over.

Maria von Wedemeyer set about looking for her fiancé. It took her several weeks to discover that he had been killed only days before freedom came to the camp he was in. Karl and Paula Bonhoeffer were the last to learn what had happened to their youngest son.

Dietrich's gift of a book did reach his friend George Bell with his final message of a life lived in steadfast faith.

18

A Lasting Legacy

On August 22, 1996, Ecumenical News International released a report from Berlin, Germany. A court there had ruled that Dietrich Bonhoeffer, executed for treason, was innocent of the charge. A law in 1946, shortly after the close of the war, had annulled Nazi judgments in general. The Berlin court in 1996 specifically exonerated Dietrich Bonhoeffer by name.

Regardless of what the courts thought of Dietrich Bonhoeffer in 1946 or fifty years later, he left an astounding personal and professional legacy. This is especially remarkable because he was only thirty-eight when he died. He carried books with him all the way to Flossenburg. He was working on a theological manuscript that he never got to finish writing. Dietrich Bonhoeffer never stopped thinking, never stopped experiencing the life God put before him. We can only imagine the impact he might have made on the Christian church in the twentieth century if he had lived another thirty or forty years.

Professionally, Dietrich Bonhoeffer was a German theologian in a period of time when German theologians were opening up a can of worms, so to speak. In the early decades of the twentieth century, German theologians such as Karl Barth, Rudolph Bultmann, and Paul Tillich challenged long-held theological interpretations and presented the world with their own theological ideas. Who was Jesus Christ and how is He relevant to the world today? What does it mean that the Bible is the Word of God? How does God make himself known to humans? Dietrich Bonhoeffer knew and respected these theological thinkers. He did not agree with everything they taught, but he respected them tremendously and was academically qualified to interact with them on these questions. He could hold his own in any academic discussion. Barth, Bultmann, and Tillich are leading names in a school of thought that came to be known as "liberal" theology. Bonhoeffer was a student of liberal theology but also rooted himself very deeply in historic Christianity. In his opinion, nineteenth-century theologians had led the church away from its historic roots, and "liberal" theologians in the twentieth century were trying to lead it back by rediscovering the meaning of the historic positions.

For his part, Dietrich Bonhoeffer consistently pressed for concrete expression of theology. Clearly the church was an important theme to Bonhoeffer. He gave both his professional life and personal life with a passion so that the church of Christ could be what God wants it to be. Just as Christ incarnates the presence of God, the church gives life to the presence of Christ in the world.

Bonhoeffer also held the Bible in high regard. While liberal theologians debated the question of what it means that the Bible is the Word of God, Dietrich Bonhoeffer acted on his simple but genuine conviction that the Bible is the Word of God. Throughout all his writings, we see his reverence for the Bible and his belief that what the Bible says is relevant to Christians in everyday situations. The Bible was not irrelevant to the kind of extreme ethical decisions Bonhoeffer faced. Rather, he turned to the pages of his Bible when he wanted guidance in those difficult decisions. Everything he wrote, even personal letters in the last weeks of his life, was infused with his comprehensive knowledge of the Bible. He said repeatedly that the Bible alone was the answer to the questions we ask. If we do not find the answers, then we must ask the questions more persistently and read the words of Scripture with more humility. He had a lifelong habit of prayer and meditation on the Word of God.

So how could a pastor with such devout personal piety join a conspiracy to take the life of the leader of his own country? Dietrich Bonhoeffer reached a point where the real question was how could he *not* join such a conspiracy? Surely this was the most difficult decision he ever faced. And even after he had made this decision, he could not speak openly about it lest he risk the lives of people around him who did not agree but who might be in danger just by knowing Bonhoeffer. In his most personal writings we see the journey that Bonhoeffer made to this decision of choosing the lesser of two evils. Bonhoeffer wrestled with the meaning of responsibility and guilt. In the end, he was convinced that an individual cannot set personal innocence over the responsibility of acting on behalf of others who are suffering. Because of Hitler's extreme policies, Jews by the millions were being murdered. If Bonhoeffer sat by and did nothing to stop the massive Nazi machinery that was killing the Jews and invading the Christian church, he would be innocent of killing Hitler. But he would be guilty of turning his back on suffering. He believed that Christians had a responsibility to stop the evil that Hitler represented. Christians are called to compassion for those who are suffering; they must act to stop the cause of the suffering. As the months and years marched on, it was clear that only the death of Hitler would stop the evil that had overtaken Germany.

For Bonhoeffer, it was not acceptable to remain personally innocent of taking Hitler's life if protecting his conscience this way meant not carrying out the disciple's responsibility to act on behalf of those who were suffering. Bonhoeffer believed that God demands responsible action and promises forgiveness to anyone who becomes guilty of sin in the process of carrying out responsible action. He believed without a doubt that God could and would bring good out of evil.

Although *The Cost of Discipleship* was one of Bonhoeffer's earliest works, its theme characterized how he lived his life. He did not just talk about theology; he lived it. He did not just talk about the relationship between faith and works; he lived out his faith in his actions. His interest in theology was always in how to live out faith in the real world. We are formed spiritually by what happens to us in our lives. From Dietrich Bonhoeffer's example of faith lived out in action in a time of personal and national crisis, we can learn valuable lessons for our lives.

First, Dietrich Bonhoeffer maintained an unfailing discipline of reading the Bible, meditating on its words and meaning, and praying for others. He believed in the importance of these habits so much that he created a community at Finkenwalde that exemplified them. The young men who were his students would not be equipped to be pastors if they left Finkenwalde only with textbook theology. They must also have developed personal spiritual disciplines and habits. When he was arrested, Dietrich might have despaired and believed that God had failed to protect him. And certainly as events pointed more and more surely toward execution, he might have wondered why God did not intervene to save him.

Instead, Dietrich persisted in reading his Bible and praying. He was never nearer to God than during those prison years when his life seemed most hopeless. Bonhoeffer did not judge the quality of his life by his circumstances but by his deep and abiding relationship with Jesus Christ.

Second, Bonhoeffer believed in the faith community, the active, visible church. In his thinking the church was not only an invisible union of believers but also a visible, concrete, active gathering of believers. God did not create people to live in isolation but in relationship with each other. The work of the believer is service to others. Dietrich fought passionately for this in the creation of the Confessing Church, believing that the church is the body of Christ, not a tool of the state. As other Confessing Church leaders were tempted to go along with objectionable regulations, Bonhoeffer consistently pressed for the church to stand apart from the flow of culture. The faith community must not give in to the whims of culture or politics, but faithfully represent the message of Jesus Christ in that cultural context.

And third, Bonhoeffer's example teaches us to enter into the sufferings of other people with courage and conviction. Feeling sorry that someone else is hurting is not enough. Christians must take public action to alleviate the sufferings of others. Discipleship is an everyday activity that takes courage and means making difficult decisions. Dietrich Bonhoeffer was not satisfied to hold the position that Jews were being treated unjustly. He believed that he must do something to stop the injustice, even at the risk of personal loss. Acting from this conviction led Bonhoeffer to the difficult decision to involve himself in an assassination plot. It was not for personal gain that he took this risk, but because he believed he was putting into action the heart of the gospel. He was willing to pay the cost of discipleship.

APPENDIX 1

Key Dates in the Life of Dietrich Bonhoeffer

1906   Dietrich Bonhoeffer is born on February 4 in Breslau, in eastern Germany

1920   Decides to study theology and become a minister

1927   Completes dissertation titled "Communion of Saints" at age twenty-one

1928   Becomes assistant pastor of a German congregation in Barcelona, Spain

1930   Moves to New York to study at Union Theological Seminary; becomes involved with the Abyssinian Baptist Church in Harlem; experiences personal conversion

1931   Begins teaching at the University of Berlin; is ordained

1933   Hitler comes to power in Germany; Bonhoeffer writes essay "The Church and the Jewish Question" (April); turns down an invitation to pastor a church in Berlin and moves to London to pastor two German congregations

1934   Becomes a founding member of the Confessing Church; withdraws from the German Evangelical Church

1935	Returns to Germany and begins teaching at Finkenwalde Seminary
1936	Gives lectures during Olympic Games in Berlin
1937	The Himmler Decree shuts down the Finkenwalde Seminary
1938	Bonhoeffer is introduced to leaders of an underground conspiracy against Hitler
1939	Goes to Union Theological Seminary in New York to teach; immediately decides to return to Germany
1940	Forbidden to speak in public; begins working as an agent for military intelligence against Hitler
1941	Forbidden to publish his works
1942	Operation Seven helps a group of Jews escape to Switzerland
1943	Engaged to marry Maria von Wedemeyer (January); plot to assassinate Hitler fails (February); Bonhoeffer is arrested (April)
1944	An attempt on Hitler's life fails (July); conspiracy exposed; Hitler orders death of everyone associated with the plot
1945	Dietrich Bonhoeffer is hanged, April 9

APPENDIX 2

Glossary

Abwehr: the official German agency for military intelligence and espionage. During Bonhoeffer's time, the Abwehr was led by Admiral Wilhelm Canaris, who used the agency to oppose Hitler.

Abyssinian Baptist Church: an African-American congregation in Harlem, New York, that Bonhoeffer became involved with while he was a student at Union Theological Seminary. Here he had personal experience with racial prejudice in North America and began to think about a similar problem in Germany.

Aryan Paragraph: church order designed to prevent non-Aryans from becoming ministers or religious teachers.

Barmen Declaration: a document that Bonhoeffer helped to write for a gathering of church leaders in Barmen, Germany. This declaration gave birth to the Confessing Church in Germany by stating its position against the government's attempt to take over the Christian church.

Bell, George: Bishop of Chichester, England, who became a lifelong friend of Dietrich Bonhoeffer. Bell worked for many years in international circles to influence world leaders to take action against Hitler and protect the German people.

Confessing Church: the German church established by leaders who withdrew from the official German Evangelical Church because of the acceptance of discrimination against converted Jews in pastoral positions and government attempts to influence church decisions.

Dohnanyi, Hans von: Bonhoeffer's brother-in-law who worked for the Abwehr and recruited Bonhoeffer to join the military intelligence agency in order to work against Adolf Hitler.

Ecumenical Movement: a group of churches from many countries that wanted to work together for a more peaceful world.

Finkenwalde: the seminary for training pastors for the Confessing Church.

Flossenburg: the Nazi camp where Dietrich Bonhoeffer was executed.

German Evangelical Church: the official Christian church in Germany at the time of Bonhoeffer. Hitler placed Nazis in key leadership positions in the church in order to control the church as well as the politics of Germany.

Gestapo: German secret police organization that worked for Hitler. Gestapo police were known for their violence against people who did not support Adolf Hitler, especially getting rid of "undesirable" people.

Jewish Question: The debate in German churches

about how to respond to Hitler's policies of discrimination and persecution of Jews. Churches debated whether they should be concerned only with Christian Jews or with helping all people of Jewish descent.

Nuremberg Laws: Nazi rulings that eliminated civil rights for Jews and treated them as non-people.

Operation Seven: a successful effort by the Resistance to help fourteen Jews escape from Germany to Switzerland in 1942. Evidence that linked Bonhoeffer to Operation Seven led to his arrest the next year.

Resistance: organized, secret work to oppose Hitler. Bonhoeffer joined the Resistance in 1939, using his international ecumenical contacts to seek support for the Resistance's efforts to overthrow Hitler.

Steglitz: a city in Germany where leaders of the Confessing Church wrestled with whether or not to give in to government pressure.

Tegel: the military prison where Dietrich Bonhoeffer stayed in Cell 92 for almost two years.

APPENDIX 3

Popular Books by Dietrich Bonhoeffer

The Cost of Discipleship

Bonhoeffer's most famous work, *The Cost of Discipleship,* was first published in 1939. The book is a rigorous exposition of the Sermon on the Mount in Matthew 5–7 and Matthew 9:35–10:42. Bonhoeffer's major concern was "cheap grace." He believed that Jesus taught a "costly grace." Jesus sacrificed His life to redeem human beings; there was nothing easy about His sacrifice. Being a disciple of Jesus means obeying His commandments, no matter what the cost. True grace brings redemption and transforms lives.

In contrast, "cheap grace" brings chaos and destruction. Agreeing to a belief mentally without a real transformation in the sinner's life is cheap grace. People want to be saved from going to hell but don't want to truly become disciples of Jesus and change the way they think and live. Simply agreeing with the teaching of the church too easily becomes a substitute for knowing the Living Christ. This cheapens the meaning of discipleship. The true believer must resist cheap grace. The Christian must rise and follow Christ obediently, even when this means standing up against cultural or political forces. An individual can do this only by knowing the true Christ, not just the teachings of the church.

Life Together

This book grew out of Bonhoeffer's experience teaching at the Finkenwalde Seminary, which he helped to found to train pastors for the new Confessing Church. Bonhoeffer strove to create a community that practiced spiritual disciplines of daily Bible reading, meditation, and prayer. Bonhoeffer's passion for Christian community fills the pages of this very brief book. He begins by outlining the meaning of true Christian community, grounded in a shared experience of Christ. Then he discusses how daily life is shared with others living together in community around the foundations of Scripture and prayer. However, Bonhoeffer recognizes that the individual Christian needs personal time to be alone and nurture an individual relationship with Christ. People should not come to Christian fellowship as a distraction from their problems, but in the strength of having been alone with God.

Letters and Papers From Prison

World War II presented reasonable people with unreasonable situations. Dietrich Bonhoeffer was one of those people, and he wrote to share with others what he learned from his personal struggles. In the letters and other papers he wrote while in prison, Bonhoeffer identified the evils of his times, especially evils that arose from the war. He warned against being deceived by evil that is disguised as good. Some of his letters reported on atrocities of war and horrors of life in prison camp. Bonhoeffer faced death daily for several years. Ironically this is just what helped him to understand the miracle of life every day that he lived. Facing death daily can lead to seeing life as the gift of God that it is. Outward circumstances do not define the quality of life or relationships.

Despite optimism about being released from prison, Bonhoeffer always knew it was possible that he would eventually be executed. His writings from prison reflected this awareness. Even from behind prison walls he could empathize with the problems faced by Christians living in turbulent, difficult times. Personal choices came at high cost.

Ethics

Bonhoeffer's *Ethics* is his major contribution to Christian theology. Bonhoeffer planned a series of lectures that he was never able to deliver. The Christian is a new creation, whose chief desire should be to please God. Human beings cannot determine what is good or evil. Only God can do that. When Adam and Eve sinned in the Garden of Eden, their perfect relationship with God was ruptured, and humans were no longer capable of discerning good and evil.

Christians should be concerned with living the will of God rather than finding a set of rules to follow. World War II was raging at the time that Bonhoeffer wrote this work. Christians faced enormous ethical decisions. Not all Christians agreed on what was the right response to the dilemmas they encountered. Believers found themselves on opposite sides of many questions. Bonhoeffer did not believe it was a simple matter to determine right and wrong in those circumstances, either on an individual level or on a national level. He only advised believers to turn to Christ for answers. Life is complicated. Bonhoeffer called for believers to humbly submit to the will of God in complicated circumstances with a life of repentance and prayer.

After Bonhoeffer's death, his student and friend Eberhard Bethge pieced together fragments of the *Ethics* manuscript that survived. Bonhoeffer was never able to complete and edit the manuscript himself.

Endnotes

Chapter 1

1. Sabine Leibholz-Bonhoeffer, *The Bonhoeffers: Portrait of a Family* (New York: St. Martin's Press, Inc., 1971), 9–10.

Chapter 2

1. Liebholz-Bonhoeffer, 9–10.
2. Ibid., 39.
3. Ibid., 9–10.
4. Eberhard Bethge, *Dietrich Bonhoeffer: A Biography* (Minneapolis: Augsburg Fortress, 2000), 27.

Chapter 3

1. Bethge, 109.
2. Ibid., 134–35.
3. Ibid., 202–204.

Chapter 4

1. Bethge, 266.
2. Ibid., 202–205.

Chapter 5

1. H. Mau and H. Krausnick, *German History 1933–1945* (London: Oswald Wolff Publishers Ltd., 1978), 16–17.
2. Ibid., 18–19.

3. Bethge, 263.
4. Mau and Krausnick, 33.
5. Bethge, 275.
6. Ibid., 276.
7. Ibid., 298.

Chapter 6

1. Joachim Fest, *Plotting Hitler's Death: The Story of the German Resistance*, trans. Bruce Little (New York: Henry Holt and Company, 1994), 49–50.
2. Mau and Krausnick, 71.

Chapter 7

1. Bethge, 429–30.
2. Ibid., 427.
3. Ibid., 441.
4. Ibid., 488.
5. Ibid., 496.

Chapter 8

1. Ruth-Alice von Bismark and Ulrich Kabitz, eds., trans. John Brownjohn, *Love Letters From Cell 92: The Correspondence between Dietrich Bonhoeffer and Maria von Wedemeyer 1943–1945* (Abingdon Press: Nashville, Tenn., 1992), 305.
2. Ibid., 306.
3. Bethge, 533ff.
4. Ibid., 538.
5. Ibid., 539.
6. Thomas Fuchs, *The Hitler Fact Book* (Los Angeles: Fountain Books, 1990), 137.
7. Bethge, 536–37.

Chapter 9

1. Bethge, 577–78.
2. Ibid., 583.
3. Robert Weldon Whalen, *Assassinating Hitler:*

Ethics and Resistance in Nazi Germany (Selinsgrove: Susquehanna University Press, 1993), 131.
4. Bethge, 637–38.

Chapter 10

1. Liebholz-Bonhoeffer, 98–99.
2. Fuchs, 149.
3. Bethge, 631.
4. Ibid., 625.

Chapter 11

1. Bethge, 672.

Chapter 12

1. Bethge, 675.
2. Ibid., 681.

Chapter 13

1. Bethge, 730.

Chapter 14

1. Whalen, 124–30.
2. Bethge, 778ff.
3. Ibid., 783.

Chapter 15

1. Bismarck and Kabitz, 38.
2. Ibid., 55.
3. Ibid., 87.
4. Bethge, 846–48.
5. Bismarck and Kabitz, 134.
6. Bethge, 654–55.

Chapter 16

1. Fest, 257ff.
2. Bismarck and Kabitz, 259.

Chapter 17

1. Bethge, 927–28.